My Troubled Life

From Trinidad and Tobago to
the Virgin Islands and America

by

Mervyn Vincent Patrick
in collaboration with
Kofi Quaye

Bloomington, IN  Milton Keynes, UK

authorHOUSE

AuthorHouse™
1663 Liberty Drive, Suite 200
Bloomington, IN 47403
www.authorhouse.com
Phone: 1-800-839-8640

AuthorHouse™ UK Ltd.
500 Avebury Boulevard
Central Milton Keynes, MK9 2BE
www.authorhouse.co.uk
Phone: 08001974150

This book is a work of non-fiction. Unless otherwise noted, the author and the publisher make no explicit guarantees as to the accuracy of the information contained in this book and in some cases, names of people and places have been altered to protect their privacy.

First published by AuthorHouse 11/1/2006

ISBN: 1-4259-1859-X (sc)

Printed in the United States of America
Bloomington, Indiana

This book is printed on acid-free paper.

I failed to succeed because I did not have a plan

The men who fail to plan…. plan to fail

Table of Contents

FOREWORD

My aim in writing this book is to provide my children with much needed information about my life and how it impacted their lives. They are the kind of children every parent should be proud of and I am very proud. Indeed, they are the main source of my inspiration as well as motivation in undertaking this onerous task of documenting my life history in a way that explains my life in ways I couldn't do otherwise.

First of all, I acknowledge, my first born, United States Marine Gunnery Sergeant, Chris M. Patrick: my other sons Wesley and Abu, and my daughter, Kurl. They have given me the rare gift of inspiring me to do this. It is as much about them as it is about me, in the sense that our lives have been naturally and necessarily intertwined over the years.

I also must acknowledge my other two sons who, to the best of my knowledge, reside in New Jersey or at this time may be living anywhere within the United States of America. I humbly ask for their forgiveness for my absence in their lives.

I also beg for the forgiveness of my ex-wife Curleen, the mother of my first four beautiful children. I acknowledge Hazel, the mother of my two sons in New Jersey. I am truly sorry for the way things turned out in our relationships.

Let it be known that I have forgiven the people that have hurt me. I give special thanks to the people that have helped me to become the person I am today. The people who are included in this category are all my teachers at the San Fernando Boys RC School and at the Mon Repos RC School. Ms. Muriel Donawa Davidson and Mr. Long are two teachers that I give special reference and thanks for their help.

I also have to include Mrs. Leah Padilla, of St Croix, Brother Ferdinand Stanislaus of St Lucia, and Sister Margaret of Dominica, all of whom I met in St Croix during my stay there between January of 1993 and November of 1994.

I thank you all for your prayers. I give my utmost respect and thanks to Pastor Leon Stutsman of Dayton, Ohio for his prayers. My respect also goes to Mr. John E Sharts, Attorney at Law and Judge in Springboro, Ohio for his understanding and kindness. I appeared before him at one time charged with driving with a suspended driver's license, and he was very lenient and showed a great deal of compassion in his administration of justice towards me. He fined me and then he turned right around and helped me to clean up my driving record, which involved going out of his way in making contact with a few States which I had driving offences in, and helping to bring closure to these offenses. Because of his actions I have a clean driver's license today.

I will be forever grateful to Mr. Earl G. Robinson, Mr. Kelvin Halls, Ms. Fran Rice, Mr. Erroll Cud Joe, Mr. Leon Charles, Mr. Carl Smith; all of these people have helped me at some point in my early life, not forgetting Mr. Harold Mc Nish, and my two brothers, Tony and Dennis Patrick.

Like most brothers, we didn't always get along but I, as well as they, knew that I could rely on their help when it counted. Many thanks to the Librarians at the Central Library, Syracuse; the people at the down town branch are highly regarded for their assistance in helping me put this manuscript together.

Gary, Linda, Wanda, and Scott are names that I remember. Not leaving out my two friends, Trevor and Vernon La Rode, two brothers who always extended a helping hand to me when I needed it; of the two I will always consider Vernon as my best friend.

INTRODUCTION

For over forty years, I have lived the life of an immigrant. I have traveled all over the Caribbean, lived in America and faced the challenges that most immigrants have to deal with. I believe that I have overcome the obstacles and that I had been privileged to benefit from the opportunities that came with those obstacles and experiences.

At least, that's what I think. It means that I have first hand experience in what immigration is all about. It also means that I had undergone the transition from being a naïve foreigner who began the journey with preconceived notions about what life overseas was—most of which turned out to be false—to one who considers himself hip and attuned to the ways of the world. In those forty years, many milestones have been reached: raising children, nurturing a marriage, a divorce and redemption. All I can say is; I have evolved through a number of different stages; as a husband, father, and entrepreneur.

I have gained enough insight into the world to be able to write about my immigrant experience in a context that allows me to discuss the political, social, and economic ramifications of the immigrant experience for Third World residents. My protracted sojourn in the United States and elsewhere was not contemplated from the beginning, but like most Immigrants, I miscalculated what I thought I would be faced with, right from the beginning.

I left my country firm in my conviction that I would return home within a short time, perhaps no more than five to ten years at the most, in a rather successful way.

I envisioned that I would make a triumphant return back home, loaded with American dollars; I figured I would be in a position to buy a new car, and have a brand new house, built with funds I had wired in from America. I would also have advanced educational credentials and cash in the bank to start a business, if I decided to. Those plans were a gross miscalculation on my part. Indeed, it has been the biggest miscalculation in my life. Little did I know that life for an immigrant is a lot more complicated, frustrating and difficult than it seems when you first begin to think about leaving your country to go abroad.

I am presently still living and working in the United States of America, some forty years after I left my native country of Trinidad and Tobago with all those great plans, all premised on the notion that I would make a fortune and return home to help my family. It did not quite work out the way that I thought it would, after years of frustration and trying, and of hanging in there.

I have decided to go with the flow and don't yearn as much to want to achieve the things I thought I would have achieved and to go back home to impress my family and friends with my fortunes. I believe that since it hasn't happened yet, and now that I am well into my sixties, I would rather share my experiences with others, in the hope that they might learn from my life story and avoid the mistakes I have made.

I could easily have called it quits and gone back home a long time ago, but what would I have been going back to? Packing up and going back home would have meant nothing less than starting all over again. I might even have had to reeducate myself in the ways of my people back home. I didn't. The prospect of re-inventing myself is not a particularly appealing proposition at this stage of my life.

The initial mistake has nothing to do with the decision I made to leave my country; it has everything to do with the projections I made with regards to my own expectations. Again, I was operating on certain assumptions that proved to be baseless. My experience and expectations in this sense are not unlike that of most immigrants from the Third World who come to America.

At the time of my emigrating to St Croix and America, it was supposed to be a temporary move during which time I would educate myself, work for a brief period and exit just as quickly as I entered. Little did I know that living as an immigrant was a lot more complicated, much more involved, that the immigrant life in general couldn't be contemplated in advance by me or, I would think, by anyone. At least, not by ordinary immigrants such as myself who undertake the journey without the means to make plans on precisely what one would do and have the wherewithal to implement those plans.

I know that I am not alone in this predicament, which is exactly what it is, nothing short of a dilemma whose solution eludes many. For the immigrant, especially those from the Third World, immigration is supposed to be no more than a passing phase; a means to an end. Going away to a foreign land is nothing less than finding a means to improve one's lot in life. The purpose is not to integrate into the society into which we immigrate. The main purpose of the immigrant's mission and immigration for most people is to get a job, make some money, save some of it and return to their native countries having adequately prepared themselves through their sojourn abroad to enjoy a better life at home.

CHAPTER 1

SEARCHING FOR ANSWERS

Can a man be born with a curse on his head or a light on him, as it is referred to in my native Trinidad culture? Are the spirits of the underworld or the evil forces powerful enough to follow a man on his journey into a country in the New World such as the United States and make his life a mess, throughout his life in the country he chooses to reside in? Can a man be forced to believe in the power of Voodoo, as he reels from job problems to failed marriages to what can generally be described as a troubled life?

If my culture, my past and my family experiences are to be believed, then I am such a person. My life has been one of misery, pain and suffering, and as I ponder the inevitable-my mortality- I can only wonder as to if it is indeed true that unseen, dark forces have controlled my entire life. The aim of this dark force was to do things to me or make me do things that would embarrass my family and myself and cause us nothing but grief and pain.

Was my belief system the reason why I failed at almost every thing I attempted, for instance the belief, that I had a curse on me, one that would make me an underachiever for the rest of my days?

It all began when I was born on March 27, 1939 in San Fernando, Trinidad to Enid Lewis and Merrick Patrick. I was the first child in a marriage that was rocky, unstable and destructive to my mother. They had been married for about a year when I came along. I don't remember anything about my life until we were living in Rose Hill, Laventille in Port of Spain.

My father was born in Grenada, a small island in the Caribbean, some ninety miles north of Trinidad and Tobago. Dad came from an educated family who was well known in Grenada, and Cariacou. I never met my father's parents and I suppose it was because they never came to Trinidad.

When I was a boy, my aunts always used to tell me that I was following in the footsteps of my father, and I believe what they were saying was based on what they heard. Rumor had it my father was hurt by people he had wronged when he was a young man in Grenada and those people had sought the help of the witch doctor to put a curse on my father…a curse that would stay with him until he died. True or false, I don't know and perhaps will never know, but it certainly looks like there was an element of truth in it because my father kept getting in trouble time and time again.

He was an educated man and had the potential to become a lot more successful. On the contrary, his life was nothing short of tragic and a big mess. For no reason at all; at least, his misfortunes couldn't be easily explained, so what are we supposed to conclude?

Voodoo? Yes, indeed. It had to be. And if this was the case, I, as the first-born was in some serious trouble. I heard the burdens and courses sins of the father get passed on to the children, according to the Voodoo traditions and mythology.

I am inclined to believe my aunts sensed, perhaps saw something there. Hence the reason they kept telling me I was like my father. With this in mind, I continue to pray that my children wouldn't suffer for the wrongs that I have done. They don't deserve it.

My mother was born in San Fernando some time in April of 1920. She was about five feet three inches tall with beautiful long black hair flowing down to her waist making her have a Hispanic look. I couldn't locate her father or anyone who had seen him so I couldn't verify her Spanish blood.

My grand mother is also gone so there is no way for me to know if she was truly half Spanish. My mother had a fiery temper and she flew off the handle quickly if her feelings were hurt, and could have a sharp tongue, yet she was a kind and generous person. Others tell me she loved to party. I know she was a very good dancer because I have seen her in action.

In spite of whatever was said about her, I loved my mother and I trusted her with my life. She told me she was made to do all the housework while her sisters were pampered. She said she wanted to get out of her mother's house by any means necessary and she got her wish when my father came on the scene. They started dating and he wanted to marry her. The marriage was approved but no one really knew who my father was and little did my mother know that she was jumping from the pot into the fire.

Her life changed when her name was changed from Enid Lewis to Mrs. Enid Patrick. I was three months old when my father went to prison. As a result, I had no christening party. My mom was devastated and embarrassed by the situation, but there was nothing she could do about it. Dad was gone for five years, depriving me of the father son bonding at a very crucial time in my life and there was nothing any one could do about it.

CHAPTER 2

ROSE HILL LAVENTILLE, PORT OF SPAIN, TRINIDAD AND TOBAGO

The year was 1945 and we lived in Rose Hill Laventille, north east of Port of Spain in Trinidad. I was six years old at the time. My mother told me when my dad was released from prison he moved the family from San Fernando to Rose Hill in Port of Spain. We were at the corner of Ovid Alley and Rose Hill. This area was always busy with people and our neighbors always visited.

I remember names like Jap and Copperhead and the Band-field brothers. We lived in the rear room of a house; the front of which faced Rose Hill road and it was there I fell in love with Steel Band music, because the Desperadoes Steel Band was located on Ovid Alley. The upper-class people in the country did not accept the Steel Pan music, at that time, because they claimed it bred violence amongst the band members and it was also very noisy and they claimed it was making no contribution to the world of music.

Today we can look back and know that they were wrong. Our room was twenty by twenty and was split by a blind partition that separated the room in two. My brother Tony and I slept on the floor on one side and there was a table and chair close to the door and also a bed on the other side of the screen. There was hardly any space to turn around.

The window on the Ovid Alley side of the house was my favorite spot to hang out because I could see and hear everything that went on in the area. The kitchen was on the outside of the house and there was also an outhouse toilet, just a few feet behind the kitchen. None of these amenities were connected to the main house.

When the rain fell this area was always muddy and dirty. In the Rose Hill area, there were immigrants from Grenada, Barbados, St Vincent, with a few families from Dominica, St Lucia and Guyana; with the majority coming from Grenada and Cariacou. During this time I was enrolled in a kindergarten school run by Teacher Stella. She was a kind and wonderful person.

I was a regular performer in her school plays and she was a beautiful person to be around. I, on the other hand, had a father I did not know. I realized that there was no bonding between my father and I; as far as I was concerned, the man who called himself my father could have been anybody.

But my mother said he was my father, and that was it; case closed. In those days kids just followed the program, and did what they were told. When I started having a relationship with my father, he was nice at first and I was beginning to like him. He bought a new bicycle for us and he would always take my brother Tony and myself for rides. I loved it, but all that changed when he started beating my mother. Then he started beating me while teaching me my schoolwork. Whenever I got stuff wrong, he got mad. During this time, I started to fear him.

He had an Indian friend called Fredrick who I truly liked; Frederick was a small man with a wonderful smile that showed his gold teeth. Whenever he came to our house he would sit me on his lap and he would tell my father what a nice boy I was. My father always replied saying that I had more tricks than a monkey. I thought that perhaps my father was seeing a lot of himself in me.

Fredrick's wife was named Yvonne. She was of African descent and a very good looking woman, but I disliked her because I learnt that she was disloyal to Fredrick with a man named Brooks Band-field. I used to wonder why my father was always beating my mother. I knew she had a sharp tongue, but was that the real and only reason? Or was he just a mean person? That scenario did not last very long because my mother suddenly left our house on Rose Hill Laventille. I believed that my mother had had enough of my father's abuse, and so she left him. In so doing, she also left me, and my brother, Tony behind. She told me later that my father threatened her to harm her if she ever took his children away from him.

Fredrick's wife Yvonne was our baby sitter, but I felt very uncomfortable with her because she was sexually abusing me whenever I was alone with her. I can still remember what she was doing to me and I wonder whether she was doing the same thing to my late brother Tony. I have never inquired from him while he was still alive. Band-field would come to pick her up in his car; they would go up and park in the Stone Quarry where they would be hugging and kissing right in front of us. My father was working at the Queens Park Hotel at this time, but he ran afoul with the law again, and my brother Tony and I were in some serious shit once again. Our father went to prison again: my mother was somewhere in San Fernando.

My brother Tony and I ended up in the hands of people who did not care for us. Suddenly our mother came to our rescue, she somehow got word in San Fernando that my father was arrested and she came for us. We were never informed of what my father was arrested for. I was glad to see my mother but she was soon in danger, because Mr. Brooks Band-field had my father's bicycle and she made the mistake of trying to take the bike from him.

Band-field slapped my mother, and she fell to the ground. He then grabbed her by her hair, which flowed down to her waist, with one hand and my father's bike in the other and dragged her on her heels. I remembered looking at the crowd of people who had gathered and everyone was laughing I held on to my brother Tony's hand crying while following our mother everywhere. Band-field continued to drag her. I cannot remember how it ended. I remember my mother telling me later on that my father's brother was there, but he did not lift a finger to help her. I suppose he was afraid of the Band-field clan. I heard every one was.

I promised to kill my father, and Brooks Band-field for what they did to my mother. I became very protective of her throughout the rest of her life, even to the point were people started calling me a Mama's boy, but I didn't care. I loved my mother and would have done anything to protect her. After the horrible experience with Bandfield, we went to live in Brown Lane in San Fernando.

CHAPTER 3

BROWN LANE, SAN FERNANDO

We lived in Brown Lane, San Fernando and the Shipley's were our next-door neighbors. There was also the Cheeseman family on the opposite side of the road. It was assumed that they were mulattos. The Cox family also lived on Brown Lane, the Nelsons with Raddy, and Neville also lived in the area and then there were the Patterson's with Skipper and Frank. Frank came to my rescue in Virginia in 1973 and I will never forget the brother's kindness. Mr. Patterson rode a big motorbike. I believe it was a Harley Davidson. It was the first motorbike that I had ever seen. The Monsegues family also lived on Brown Lane.

Our apartment was full with aunts, cousins, and uncles: my cousin Kendrick was born there. It was not unusual in those days for a family to be living in close proximity to each other. Hazel Shipley and I played Dolly House there under the table in our apartment. We were in the same age group.

At this point, I was fatherless again. Close to Brown Lane was the Free French Steel Band with Zola as Captain. My uncle Joseph (Shirley) Atwell was a member as well as a very talented Pan-man named Theo Black James. The Rostant family lived close by.

Mazin Rostant was my grandmother Mary's sister; they all spoke patois. The Rostant family lived at the Roy Joseph Housing complex: also in the same complex lived the popular Trinidadian singer, Mr. Lloyd Boucher who later went on to England and made several hit records. There was also a friend of our family, a Mr. Horace James: he also went to England and became famous with his comedy show. The Rostant family later moved to Picton Road, Laventille, Port of Spain.

I love San Fernando. The library corner was, for all intents and purposes, the main square. With seven different streets converging at this point from all directions, it was the hub of the city. Harris Promenade, to me, was the handle. The real estate on the promenade was of very high value. The Methodist School, with Noel And Ashton Hayes, was a part of that block and further down the line, we had the Anglican Church, then my school, the San Fernando Boys RC, with the Catholic Church next to it.

Still further down was the San Fernando Town Hall where my mother met the world famous African American, Mr. Paul Roberson. Next to the Town Hall was the Fire Station. The San Fernando General Hospital was on the western end along with several law offices. On the other side was the police station that was built like a fort; there was a courthouse, a convent, not forgetting the Bandstand where the police band and world-famous entertainers entertained. The landscaping had huge salmon and oak trees that lined the road from the library corner to the West End. You had to be pretty rich to own property on the Promenade.

The library corner itself had rum shops, Chinese restaurants, drug stores, a movie house, a taxi stand, Roti shops, and vendors of all description, with their trays filled with plums, apples, mangoes, and sugar cakes made with grated coconut, figs, bananas, etc, etc.

As the years went by, I learned the town better than the city's mayor at the time…through walking over the hills of San Fernando, which made my legs strong. I was small in stature, a mere five feet eight inches, but I was very athletic.

Mucarapo Street is located south of the library corner; it is one of the streets that flowed into the Library Corner. On Mucarapo Street was the market with more vendors, where you got your beef, pork, fish, chicken, fruits and vegetables, all fresh; a busy marketplace it was. This was the place where I went when I was hungry, to ask for a meal or to steal something to eat. The market's busiest day was Sunday because Sunday was our biggest meal-shopping day. Mucarapo Street was also the street where you find the ladies of the night; it became one of my favorite places to visit when I reached the legal age. Mucarapo Street also had movie houses, drug stores, a Chinese laundry, as well as a few restaurants

I really loved San Fernando. The railway station was in operation in the early forties and you could travel from San Fernando to Port of Spain by train for a small fee. Everyone in the country got along fine then, although it was not perfect; Indians, Africans and their offspring from the slavery era got along well together. There were also Portuguese, Dutch, Spanish, Jews, Syrians; each ethnic group had its piece of the rock. But the lions share went to the light skinned European bourgeoisie citizens of the town. I believe that was the way it was then in Trinidad and still is today.

CHAPTER 4

MON REPOS

The family moved from Brown Lane in Port of Spain to Mon Repos/Navet Housing scheme in San Fernando. They were all new low-income family homes and our house was on the Mon Repos side. We were housed at 27 Wooding Street and most of the families who lived on Brown Lane moved to the complex, which was about ten miles east of Brown Lane.

The house in which we lived was a three-bedroom house with spacious living room, an adjourning kitchen and bath and lots of yard space. Moving to Mon Repos made my walk to San Fernando Boys RC much longer, but it was no problem; I had the energy. Mon Repos is West of Princess Town, East of San Fernando, North of Penal, and South West of Taruba Village, which was the home of many of the Indian citizens of Trinidad and Tobago. We all got along then. I will never forget the Indian woman with her milk pail on her head bringing milk to our house, all the way from Taruba Village. No one dared to disrespect her. That was a peaceful time in Trinidad and Tobago. We had families of different races and religions living at Mon Repos during that time. I loved going to the San Fernando Boys RC School. My teachers were Ms Muriel Donowa and Mr. Long. My friend, Newman Wilson, often took me to his house for lunch and his parents never seemed to mind. Newman and I were both members of the school choir; another one of our schoolmates was calypsonian The Black Stalin who later turned out to be a champion in his field.

Head teacher Mr. Charles was in charge of me; to me the man was ten feet tall, although actually he was about six feet with a broad smile that showed strong beautiful white teeth; he was kind and humble...where his humility came from, I don't know. in my view again the man could have been the ruler of any nation on the face of this planet. But I will never forget Father Sebastian, and Father Maingot, two Catholic priests who helped me form my early impression of white people. I thought all white people were just as warm and peaceful as Father Maingot and Father Sebastian. Later in my life, I discovered my early impression of white people was wrong.

San Fernando Boys RC was also the school of the boys that formed the world famous Dutchy Brothers Band. I remember Eugene; he had a strong confident look about him. There was also Orville, Ottmar, and Leo. Leo saved me from drowning one time; the place was a spot called Channel, which was north of the San Fernando Jetty where I got into trouble while swimming in the sea. These were the boys I remember from my school. There were also sisters in the family but I never knew any of them. Old man Dutchy played the saxophone with a lighted cigarette in his mouth, which was awesome to me because I have never seen any one do that. I thank you, Leo Duvluth for saving my life.

In school I was getting good at reading, writing, and math, but my love for singing was getting stronger. Mr. Long was in charge of the school choir and I always looked forward to choir practice because as a member you would sing in church, but that opportunity never came because of the family's move to Mon Repos. I fell in love with white folks at a very early age and I wanted to be just like them because at this time in my life I thought they did every thing that was good and clean. I thought that black people never did anything positive; mainly because most of the books we were reading in school never showed any blacks doing any thing in a positive light. Thanks to the man, Clement 'Clemmy' George for letting me know that was not so. He had all kinds of books about Africa and the greatness of the African people, and the beauty of their continent. Yet white writers kept writing negative things about the African continent. Mon Repos RC School was built in the early fifties the school was west of our house and just a stone throw away. There was also a church on the same property. I was enrolled in the school but there was great sadness because I was leaving my friends, Newman Wilson and the Black Stalin in my old school. The up side to the situation was Mr. Long and Mr. Charles both transferred to Mon Repos RC School. I don't remember if my teacher Ms Muriel Donowa did. My cousin Kendrick was growing nicely but I had other cousins coming from everywhere. My aunts were busy making babies and 27 Wooding Street was getting very crowded. I had cousins who are twins, Gerald and Gloria Bacchus, brother and sister to Kenrick, the brilliant Ashley, Marion, Gail, and Patricia, and on the Indian side. I have cousins Roma, Debbie, Lana and Ian. I have cousins Hazel, "Dinky" Donna, Rudy, and the brilliant Helen Codogan who went to China to teach English. Yes, we were crowded at 27 Wooding Street; we were not the Partridge family, but we all got along pretty good.

CHAPTER 5

TEACHERS

Teachers were the people we tried to emulate in my school days, and the teacher I tried most to emulate at Mon Repos RC School was Mr. Long. He rode his bike to school and was never late. He gave me good advice and he told me I had a good singing voice. I wanted to be like Mr. Long. Mr. Charles retired from Mon Repos and Mr. Chinaleong took over as head teacher.

There were several other outstanding teachers at Mon Repos RC School. One was Mr. Dulal, who whipped my butt many times when I misbehaved; Mr. Daniel who once told me I would become a good batsman, talking about cricket. There was also Mr. Cochran, Ms. Gooding, Ms. Ishmael and the charismatic Mr. Palmer who later achieved high status in the teaching profession. My very best friend at Mon Repos RC School was a student named Lloyd 'Jeff 'Lewis, a wonderful human being and a powerful defensive football soccer player.

Lloyd was about five seven but he was built like a brick shit house. We both played cricket and football for Mon Repos RC School. I was the speedy right-winger on the football team and I was also the opening batsman for the school in cricket as well, along with another friend named Ian Haynes. One student that I had great respect for was Sherwin Benjamin. The Benjamin family lived on the Naparima Mayaro Road which borders Mon Repos on the west side the Farray family also lived on the same road.

I was getting along well in school and everyone gave respect and credit to the teachers. As the years went by, I also improved in academics, excelling in cricket and football at the same time. My love for the Pan was growing during this time; I heard Theo James made a recording of a song call *Anna*; it was one of the best tenor Pan solo I have ever heard. I often wonder if he ever did make money on the recording. I still don't know.

Mon Repos RC School was coed with children of all races.. One of my classmates was a young Indian student named Bobby Mohamed who turned out to be one of Trinidad and Tobago greatest Pan men. He was a pan leader, arranger, and composer. Bobby turned the pan world upside down with his innovative style as the Captain of the Guinness Cavaliers Steel Band. He took Steel Band music to heights that no other leader in the Pan world has matched. Bobby and his all Black Pans went to Port of Spain and rocked the Pan world at panorama time. Today, I still cannot play the tenor Pan, which is my favorite instrument.

I was always getting into trouble at school, mainly for fighting. There was this one student named Constance. He was always teasing me and I responded by punching or kicking him. Some students said he was gay: I would end up in Mr. Chinaleong's office to get a whipping for striking him. What I find strange about this situation is that some fifty something years later, I married a woman named Constance.

Mon Repos RC School turned out some outstanding students as well as teachers who made it big in the global community. The brilliant Lune Alexander, a mechanical engineer, was one of those students and some say he designed part of the Hess Oil Refinery; there were still many others.

Under colonial rule there were little or no opportunities for the poorer class of people. If you were dark skinned and uneducated or without a skill, you were in serious trouble. We were very poor at 27 Wooding Street and lots of days there was nothing to eat. The cane fields was a source of food when in season or the San Fernando Hill which provides us with a variety of mangoes that were just as good. The hill was my favorite get away place with its four hundred and eighty steps. I walked those steps many times during my youth to get to the summit without even breathing heavy...today fifty steps would kill me.

Today man and his machines have obliterated the hill in the name of progress. I will never forget the book *Lady Chatterley's Lover.* Reading this book led me into my carnalistic self. I borrowed the book from Clemmy George and I went up the San Fernando Hill by way of the four hundred and eighty steps. I read the book from front to back, not missing a word. Of course there were a few interruptions during the time. The book blew my mind. I kept it for weeks hiding from Clemmy. Eventually he caught me and he told me he would never loan me another book because he was angry as hell; but the book opened my mind to sexual fantasies.

Grandpa Mr. Dennis did a lot of planting that helped the family's food bank; cassava; green-figs, corn, ochra and pigeon peas were some of the crops that brought food on the table. Grandpa whipped my butt many times but he always took me with him when it was time for plowing, planting, and reaping. Everyone thought he was my father; it was a well-kept secret that my father was in prison. Sunday meal was our best. We had Callaloo, stewed chicken, white rice with ground provision. There were no leftovers. I had no father, no mentor and my uncle Joseph "Shirley" Atwell whom I loved and respected was busy getting his own life together. He found work at the Shell oil refinery in the Deep South of San Fernando. He always encouraged me to do the right thing. He found his beautiful bride Doreen in the south. Later they went on to make a beautiful family.

I was practically raising myself, and developing bad habits. I was mostly lying and stealing but I knew I wanted to be somebody or something. The road I was traveling at the time was only going to lead to serious trouble or death. The kids in my age group who had parental guidance were focused on their education; and most of them ended up in college. But it seemed as though I was going to end up just like my father, which was something I dreaded. As the oldest kid at the house, I ran all the errands did most of the housework and when I messed up I was punished. One of my aunts would put me to kneel on an eighteen-inch grater with a coal pot iron in each hand pointing towards the heavens...sometimes for ten to thirty minutes. Where she learned this form of punishment from, I don't know, but it was a form of punishment she never used on her children.

My aunts called me everything but nice. I was really pissing them off with my actions everyday and they called me names. I was a thief, I was worthless, I have a light on me, (meaning a curse), long face, long neck; the verbal abuses were endless and even my brothers, Tony and Dennis, were calling me names. I thought everyone hated me. I knew my mother loved me but she was whipping my butt when she came home at the end of the month from her sleep in job, so it was a bitter sweet home coming in spite of the fact that she had a few dollars in her pocket and brought us stuff.

On Wooding Street we had families such as the Joseph family with Mr. Vernon Joseph who was one time deputy Mayor of San Fernando. He was responsible for the Community Center erection at the bottom of Wooding Street. His son, Rupert helped form our soccer team, The Searchers. We had our own field for cricket and soccer. The pitch was rough and stony but we played some exciting games on the surface; both cricket and football; we had good teams in both sport.

Also on Wooding Street there was the Nelson family with Selywn and Ossie. Their father, Mr. Nelson always complimented me on my singing voice especially when I did my Satchmo Armstrong imitation. There was the Gomez family with Russell who achieved a very high position in law enforcement later on in his life. I can't forget the brilliant Kellman and my friend, master electrician and jockey, Kenrick 'Bunny' Gomez. Then there was the Peters family with my friend Conrad, a wonderful and kind person. There was the Clarkes family with, at that time the love of my life, Stephanie, but she didn't know it because I never expressed that to her because her brother, Michael was my friend. There was Burt Clark who had a voice that was very similar to Sam Cooke, there was also Leroy, his big brother. We were always throwing rocks at each other. Maybe it was because of Stephanie, I don't know.

In 1993 while working on the Hess Cat Cracker in St Croix as a welder I was having lunch with Leroy and a brother from Marabella named Rennie. I made the mistake of telling them I was writing a book Leroy laughed in my face. He said: "Who knows you; nobody knows you, and nobody will buy your book" After that day, I never sat with or spoke with Leroy again.

There were other wonderful families on Wooding Street: the Clifford's, and the Horsham's with Carl and Rennie. Carl was an outstanding athlete with great potential; he played soccer for St Benidicts College. He was strong and powerful and he was the school's goalkeeper; he was also a great sprinter. Carl earned himself a scholarship to a Southern US college and later went on to work for the United States Government. He traveled all over the world as Chief of Protocol; he has been to Russia many times, today he still holds a high position in the US government. I am extremely proud to say this man is a friend of mine. I was rubbing shoulders with young men who later in their lives made some note worthy accomplishments at the local and international levels, they all lived on Wooding Street. There were the Wilsons with my friend, Albert who later went on to England; there were the Cheesemans, the Simmons, the Georges with Cecil Carabon who also went on to England, the Williams with David and Tony, Winston, and Trevor.

Mr. Williams was a druggist who later married my friend Leslie Blackman's mother, so Leslie was, of course, God brother to the Williams boys. Leslie later became a student at the Naparima College; all the Williams boys went on to college. Today they are making great contributions in their respective professions. My friend Leslie is also doing great in his field. I will never forget the time I took Leslie's pellet gun and started playing around with it while we were hanging out on the hill at the top of Wooding Street; several of my friends were there and everyone was telling me to quit the messing around. I took the gun, and put it on my shoulder like I was a soldier. I had my finger on the trigger; I squeezed it and the pellet shot out grazing me on the side of my face. I could have killed myself playing around; I was bleeding, and I was scared. I was taken to the Fire Station for medical attention which was just a stone throw away from where we were. I still have a scar along side my right ear, a reminder that I am not supposed to fool around with guns.

Wooding Street also had the LaRode family with two of my best friends, Trevor and Vernon. We all got along as kids even though the parents kept to themselves. Lower down Wooding Street was the Nurse family the

Roaches with my friend Winston, the Charles with the outstanding Tello who later went on to Presentation College. Today, Tello is a chemical engineer as well as a, minister. Across from our house was the London house with Linda, Joan, Judy, and Charles Stewart. Linda was my honey at one time.

I have come to the conclusion that it was not a curse or a light or Voodoo, that led me in the direction that I took in life or influenced me to do the things I did throughout my life. I choose rather to believe it was a lack of parental guidance, no formal education, and no adult encouragement. I didn't have and astrological reading like they do in some countries and which is used as a blue print for the way a child's life should go. In short, the building blocks I needed for growth and development as a young man were nonexistent. After I quit Mon Repos RC school things got worse. I didn't tell anyone I intended to quit school. I woke up in the morning, got dressed for school but I went elsewhere. Sometimes I'd go through the market to steal something to eat or I would climb the four hundred and eighty steps to the summit of the San Fernando hill stay there until I knew it was time to go home. Many of my school vacations I spent in Point Fortin with my cousins, the Ferdinands. My aunt Elaine married this cool dude named Robert. To me, he was the strong silent type. I loved being in the Deep South. No one called me names here. I got along with all my cousins. Mavis, my eldest cousin, later moved to San Fernando. Owen, Carl, Gavin, Angie, Jacqueline. Majorie and Janet were all beautiful people who are living good lives. But my life was filled with uncertainty and danger and no one had any answers. Would I follow in my father's footsteps? Would the evil forces consume me? After it was discovered I had quit school, no one seemed to care. My mother thought about sending me to learn a trade but could not decide where. Unless you had a godfather in the refinery, you didn't stand a chance of getting a job there. The future didn't look very bright for my brothers and myself. I was living life one day at a time. I was very restless and very impulsive, a very dangerous combination.

CHAPTER 6

TASPO

The year was 1951. I was twelve years old. I didn't know anything in particular, but I could read and write. I was morally and spiritually weak and didn't know what morality meant. I did not have access to the books I knew existed during my school days. Additionally, the subject matter of the books I was exposed to was inferior to the standards of that time. I believe that this was one of the methods the colonial rulers used to keep Black people in darkness and ignorance.

Twirly and Twisty were two screws, and *Dan is the man in the van*, were books we were reading. I often wondered why the teachers accepted and taught this nonsense. I never found out, but I know that they certainly were not the type of books that would make kids smart. What was their motivation?

Sir Hubert Rance was the Governor of Trinidad and Tobago during this time. My love for the Steel

Band was growing, but things were falling apart in the Pan yards. There was endless violence between the musicians and the band followers. There was also progress in the form of new designs in the Steel Band instruments. Sir Hubert Rance came up with a great idea to form a National Steel Band. Band Leaders were called in from the various bands, and after several meetings TASPO was formed. The Trinidad All Steel Percussion Orchestra was comprised of present and past band members. I remembered names like Nathaniel Joseph Griffith who was a Bajan; he was educated in music and was a member of the Trinidad Police Band in earlier days. Then there was Sydney Gallop, Lennox Pierre, Nathaniel Chritchlow, and Theo BJ Stephens of the Free French Steel Band with Captain Zola in charge. The band also had names like Ellie Mannette, who was a Pan master in his own right; Winston Spree Simon, Belgrave Bonaparte and Anthony Williams were names I also remember.

TASPO was one of the best organizations formed in relationship to the Steel Pan movement. The things that happened during the Steel Band movement because of TASPO really did make a great difference. I believe that my mental state at the time had an adverse effect on me hence the reason why I still cannot play any of the Steel Pan instruments today. July 1951 was the summer festival of Britain and TASPO was booked to perform in England during the festival. There were trip stops scheduled to be made to Martinique, Paris, and London. I must give my utmost respect to Mr. Edric Connor for the help he had given the band because when they arrived in England the sea air had rusted the pans and the spectators were skeptical about whether the show would go on. I heard that when the boys started playing, everyone in the audience was very impressed. It must be mentioned here that the Band performed in aid of the Jamaican Hurricane relief fund.

I managed to get a radio at the house after a while and started listening to what was mostly British correspondents. I listened to the radio most of the time and realized that the programming was syndicated mostly for British people. There were lots of classical music; I loved Hi Neighbor with Mr. Sam Gahny. Mr. Frank Prado was my favorite show and I never missed Sunday serenade with Mr. Gahny as host; Sunday Serenade performers were Ed and Angela Johnson, Telly Maxine a wonderful vocalist, and The Strollers singing group. The show was in Port of Spain; the Georges trio from San Fernando was also a regular, not forgetting the popular Jazz piano player, Mr. Felix Roach. I loved the show so much that a few years later I ended up on Sunday Serenade as a member of the Dolphins Quartet singing group lead by the versatile Mr. Allan Nicholas, Massy and Rudy.

When my father came out of prison, my grandmother took him to see Mother Lion and the move changed his whole life. Mother Lion was the spiritual doctor in our area. They said he had a problem. He had a curse placed on him, which was invoked by people he had wronged, who had sought the medicine people to punish him for what he did. He was just a young boy living in the country of his birth Grenada and was not really responsible for his actions. He was determined to change, and so he moved to Penal, a village South of San Fernando. There he had a relationship with a wonderful woman named Isabel. She bore him two sons, Michael and Peter.   Michael passed very early in life; Peter is a minister and lives with his beautiful family in New York.

My father enrolled me in the Allen's Commercial College for shorthand and typing. The typing part was easy but the short hand side of it was kicking my butt. I often thought that that type of schooling was girl stuff. Eventually he pulled me from the course because I was not making any progress.

The year was 1955 and my father got a job at the cement factory, which was about fifteen miles north of Mon Repos in San Fernando. He was beginning to make progress in his life, but Ms Isabel passed and my father moved from Penal to St Margaret's village, one mile south of the cement factory.

The political climate was changing in Trinidad and Tobago at that time with the introduction of the People's National Movement political party led by Dr. Eric Williams. It looked like things were going to be different and that gave the people hope. The people of African descent especially were hoping change would come, but change is a slow process and the people seemed impatient.

CHAPTER 7

CARNIVAL TIME IN TRINIDAD AND TOBAGO

Carnival time in Trinidad and Tobago was a wonderful time. People came from all over the world for this festive occasion. It is similar to the New Orleans Mardi Gras but more unique because in Trinidad, we have Calypso and Steel Band music. There are parties and dances everywhere during the carnival season, leading up to the two big days before Ash Wednesday.

I want the world to know that I did the glove thing before Michael Jackson. It was a Carnival Sunday night and my cousin Lenore came to San Fernando for the Carnival. My uncle Shirley used the single white right hand glove the year before. It was a pair but he had lost one glove and a group of us were going to party at the Palms Club that night. The group included my cousin Lenore. I would wear the glove in case we got separated.

I was a dancer boy in those days, some thing I inherited from my mother who was a great dancer in her day. I literarily could dance all night and never get tired. The glove was not sequined like Michael's, but it did the job every time we were separated. I would put my gloved hand up and everyone would find me, regardless of where I was in the hall. My cousin, Lenore is the only one I remember in our group. Maybe I wore the gloves to get attention; I don't know.

We had a full house and food was scarce because all my aunts took care of their own children first. For me, it was survival by any means necessary. I had no clothes, no food, and no shoes, not even a toothbrush. I remembered my dog named Flee. I had raised him from a pup till he was full-grown. Believe me when I say that my dog made me feel like I was somebody. The things that made me insecure included poverty, no education, no family structure, no love and no mentor, but the dog drove me. I was a very angry kid at seventeen, but fun loving at the same time. I had no self-control. I was undisciplined and I was reaching out.

CHAPTER 8

CEMENT FACTORY

My father got me a job at the cement factory. My brothers and I were still living at Mon Repos and my mother was working at her sleep in job. Everyone was delighted with the fact that I was working; but it was time for us to move out of Mon Repos.

We found an apartment in Marabella, which is five miles north of Mon Repos, but closer to the cement Factory. My father had loaned me his bicycle to get to work. I rode from Mon Repos to Claxton Bay every day except on my day off. I was the big spender on payday. I took my friends to the Chinese Restaurant for food and drinks and bought clothes for myself. The cement factory job was just that—a job. I worked shift work and I was learning to become an operator in the factory. I was working alongside men like Gittens, Steadman, and the Kennedy brothers. Mr. Medford was the master carpenter. There was Rex in the machine shop; Rex tried introducing me to air conditioning repair, but I was not focusing at the time. I was leaning towards bodybuilding with the help of my cousin Rudolph 'Natty' Lewis. But I never stayed with it. I remembered supervisors like Pratt and Mitchell, none of whom I liked. I had always had affection for white people, but these two white men I stayed away from whenever I could. Like everything else, I took my job at the cement factory for granted while there. I became captain of both the football and cricket teams; I got a lot of respect from my teammates and was becoming very popular and very good at both sports; still I didn't know who I was or my purpose in life. All I know was I had energy to burn.

CHAPTER 9

MARABELLA

In Marabella, my friends were Lance and Berry, who were brothers. I was also beginning to like Glenda B. She lived across the street from us, but my favorite pleasure were the ladies of the night. I was a young man in Trinidad, good-looking, had a good job with endless potential, but I still was not satisfied and thought I did not have what I needed...a college education. What I had was the belief that I had a curse on me...one that I would die with.

In Marabella, I came into the music that I have always loved, Steel Band music. The world famous Southern Marines with Milton Lyons and the Scarlet Steel band with the talented Michael Alleyne were within my reach in Marabella; but still I stayed away from the Pan yard. My two brothers, Tony and Dennis, became members of theScarlet Steel band, but I stayed away although nothing was stopping me from becoming a member of either group. I could not understand why, nothing that I could see was responsible. What was holding me back? To this day I am still baffled about it.

I was a very laid back young man and took nothing seriously. I think I was still afraid of the so-called curse that I thought I had on me. At the same time, I was worried about the course my life was taking. I did not have a formal education and I didn't know any Scriptures. Sometime before I left Mon Repos, I had stolen a bicycle and sold it to a kid. He got caught with the bike and had to return it. He gave me dirty looks every time I saw him and I was told that his family had put a light on me...you know, Voodoo curse. These were the things that I mostly worried about because I didn't want to follow in the footsteps of my father.

After working for about two years at the cement factory, I just quit and started drinking heavily. I was in a deep state of depression. One of the clubs I gambled in threw me out and made me persona non grata. I promised myself that I would get even. One night I broke into the club and stole a few bottles of rum and some small change. The very next day I was trying to sell the rum, and didn't know some one had fingered me. There I was, standing under the almond tree on the Marabella train line with three bottles of Mount Gay rum in a bag when two men approached me. They were plain-clothes officers. I thought I had a sale but then I saw the SRP behind them and I realized that it was a trap. The SRP was the same one who had caught me trying to sneak into the movie house the week before. He was in uniform and I also recognized one of the other men as a police officer. I dropped the bag and a foot race ensued down the train line. I was much faster than they were, but I got caught hiding in some one's house. How they found me, I don't know. I was arrested and charged with breaking and entering. Once again, I had brought shame on my mother and my brothers. Because I had a clean record I was given a small fine and put on probation. Perhaps Mother Lion had a hand in my lenient sentencing because I was taken to see her many times before my court appearance. Eventually my mother sent me to Port of Spain to stay with her aunt Mazin Rostant who had moved from the Roy Joseph Housing complex in San Fernando to a home on Picton Road in Laventille.

I wondered whether the curse would follow me and I knew that only time would tell. I was welcomed at the house on Picton Road in Laventille. The house had a great view of the Gulf of Paria and the Port of Spain docks. It was a very exciting thing to see the big ships come into port. I learned that it was Uncle Eversley, a merchant seaman himself who found and bought the house. There was no running water in the house, which surprised me at first. This was the capital city of Trinidad, I said to myself, so I figured that things should be modern.

At the house there was also Aunt Mazin; who spoke French and patios. Eastlyn, my cousin, and Joe, and Jacqueline made up the rest of the household. Cousin Joe was cool and we became good friends. As the new kid at the house, I had to do my part, which was mainly to supply the house with water. The standpipe was a short walk up the hill, no more than a hundred yards, but it was up hill and provided a little strain when I fetched the water. I also had to clean the yard and do a little gardening. I was earning my keep in a few months. Because of my cousin Joe, every one grew to know me on Picton Road and called me South. I was blending in nicely with the guys on the hill. Sonny Caterson, a shoemaker, took me in hand. He was a wonderful man and he tried to teach me some things about the trade. There were lots of Grenadians living on Picton Road and we all got along fine. Maybe it was because I was part Grenadian. My girl friend was TK. I use her initials out of my respect for her. I became a member of the All Fours Club, the cricket and football teams and I was beginning to appreciate the move from Marabella to Port of Spain. I still had no plans for the future because the future was not looking bright to me at this point of my life. The People's National Movement with Prime Minister Dr Eric Williams was a Godsend to the people of Trinidad and Tobago, in my view. We were fast becoming a nation with improvements in education and public transport, etc. There were lots of improvements in the work situation in the country and revenues from our oil and gas were being used for the needs of the people.

CHAPTER 10

THE CRASH PROGRAM 59

The crash program started some time in the late fifties. It was a ten-day work for ten-day pay the government introduced to keep the people working; and to stimulate the economy of the country. Months after I arrived in Port of Spain, I got to sign on to the program because of Sonny Caterson.

He was a wonderful human.who extended a helping hand to any one in need. I worked with Toewine from Despers, Joe from the Labasse and one man named Jack Slade. Those guys had reputations as Bad Johns on the hill, but I got along with everyone. What we did basically in the crash program was to clean the sidewalks. Our tools included a hoe, cutlass, brooms; it was a no brainer.

I became very popular with the guys on the hill mainly because of my skills in both soccer and cricket. We were the Hill Stars, we were all brothers: Cephus,

Khaki Fomoa, Herman Blondell, just to name a few. Sonny Caterson tried start a Steel Band on the hill but was not successful. I had thought for sure that I would become a Pan man in his band. I was playing the bongos while learning to play the Tenor Pan. The band did not last very long because there was no funding for new Pans, and besides, most of the good Pan players went down to John John to join the Carib Tokyo band which was just down hill on the south side from us on the Picton Road.

At this stage in my life I had met a lot of good men who gave me good advice, but I was hard headed and took no advice from anyone because I didn't trust anybody. However, I met a man called Br George Bowen who was the kindest man I have ever met. He ran the Blessed Martin Welfare Association, an organization sponsored by the Catholic Church. Brother Bowen was a man of God and nothing seemed to fluster him. I would go to Bro Bowen before I went to talk to a priest. My cousin Joe and my self became members of the club. We had everything except cricket and soccer. Lloyd Joseph who was a member wrote a play about a Catholic priest named Father Murphy. It was a very good play. I got the part of Father Murphy and I was told that I did a good job playing the role. The play was even entered into the better Village competition in St Ann's, and Lloyd became very popular because of the play. Later on in 1985, I was attending broadcasting school in Manhattan, New York, when I ran into him. I was also getting involved in the Calypso world at the same time playing gigs as the MC at a Calypso show on Nostrand Avenue in Brooklyn.

Bill Trotman was there, and the Professor who I consider to be one of the world's best Pan men, was also performing. Lloyd Joseph had a high position in the Trinidad and Tobago Consul Generals office at the time, and he and some other dignitaries were in attendance. I introduced myself to Lloyd and he acted as though he didn't know me. If you are a writer or director of a play, how can you not remember your leading man; I thought. Lloyd turned out to be a big time snob. I enjoyed it at Brother Bowens place. I remembered he had a relative from Grenada that was spending time in Trinidad. She was what we call a seer woman and the word was she was good. She read my palm and told me there was a lot of trouble ahead for me. I was sorry afterwards that I allowed her to read my palm, because it scared the dickens out of me.

In the mean time, my brothers and my mom were still in San Fernando. There was little or no communication between us. For days and weeks, I tried to shake off the palm reading results. I had to fool myself by telling myself this woman didn't know what she was talking about but deep down inside I believed her. I wanted to get out of Trinidad real bad and my thoughts were of America even though most of my friends went to England. It was easy to go to England in those days but America was on my mind and I felt that if I left Trinidad I would leave the curse behind.

I was wrong. There was a serious down sizing on the crash program even though the PNM was in power. Jobs were scarce but the future looked bright. The country finally had a leader who cared for the people. We were going to become a nation and we were going to have our

Independence. I wondered if it would change any thing. Time would tell, we thought.

Uncle Eversley built a little convenience store next to the house on Picton road; I helped in the construction and things were going well. I was helping out my Uncle Eversley who had retired as a merchant seaman and decided to go into business on his own. He had helped his son, my cousin Joe, to become a seaman as well.

I was happy for Joe but I missed him when he left Trinidad in early 1960. By the end of the year Joe was back in Trinidad and he told me he didn't like the traveling at sea. In the mean time, I had broken up with my girl friend TK and was looking at another girl who I wanted to be with. I tried very hard to talk to her but she would not give me the time of day. My cousin Joe was my mediator, but Curleen Belfast would have nothing to do with me and I didn't know why.

CHAPTER 11

MY MOTHER IS BACK IN PORT OF SPAIN

My mother moved to Port of Spain some time in 1960. She had broken up with her boy friend, Tarzan. She told me my brothers Tony and Dennis had moved to the town called Vista Bella in San Fernando. It did not take my mother long to find work and soon she was working with the world famous Olive Walke of La Petite Musical, the singing choir that made Mango famous. My mother took me to meet Ms Walke and she told her that I could sing but I never had the opportunity to sing for her.

After a few months my mother quit the job and was working for another family in the same Cascade area, which was north west of Port of Spain. The Peel family was Canadian and I believe Mr. Peel was working for the Canadian Embassy. In the mean time, I was doing odd jobs here and there, in the city mostly, at the bakery on Prince Street. I did not have a skill or formal education and I wondered how far the little reading, writing and math that I knew could take me…God alone knows.

I had spoken to Uncle Eversley about getting me on a ship and he told me it would take time and that I would have to get a passport first. But that never materialized because my bad habits caught up with me once again. Uncle Eversley caught me red handed, in the cash draw. We were off-loading goods from his car into the store and I was left alone for a few minutes. I believe he was watching me closely because he knew I was a thief. He told me to get the hell out, and that very day I had to leave Aunt Mazin's house. I was very ashamed of myself. The family cried shame on me and I even heard Aunt Mazin called in the Obeah man to punish me for my crime. I started to think about what the woman told me about after she read my palm. She was right on the money. The sins of the father fall on the children. Was I following in my fathers' footsteps? On the same day I got caught stealing from Uncle Eversley store, I had to walk to my mother's job from Picton Road to Cascade.

It was a very long walk and my mother was surprised to see me. She was also disappointed in my action and it meant I had no place to stay in Port of Spain or in San Fernando. We went to see Br Bowen who advised my mother to take me to the hostel on Duncan Street in Port of Spain where a man named Nunes was running the show. I was given the rules and a bed. I don't remember the cost of my stay. I kept going back to the hill because I was still a part of the cricket and football team as well as the All Fours Club. I stayed away from the Rostant house because when the word got out of my misdeeds, I was embarrassed. It was not such a big thing to the guys, but it hurt my chances with the woman I loved. She wanted no part of me. She never looked my way but my feelings for her would not leave me.

CHAPTER 12

INDEPENDENCE FOR TRINIDAD AND TOBAGO

Trinidad and Tobago became independent on the thirty first of August 1962. It was a great day for our country. We were a nation now and our destiny was in our hands. Would it work? Time will tell, we told ourselves. There was a lot of skepticism on the part of the people who wanted our country to fail but we had a strong leader in our Prime Minister, Dr. Eric Williams and we believed that we would not fail.

The Steel Band movement benefited greatly from PNM control of Trinidad and Tobago. The violence had ceased and the different bands were getting Sponsorship from the big businesses. The future of the Steel Band movement in the country was on the up swing

I was in Woodford Square on that memorable night of our Independence along with thousands of other people when Dr. Williams said to the masses that *Massa Day* was done and the people replied with an emphatic *Yes*. It was a great time to be a citizen of Trinidad and Tobago.

By the end of 1962, I was truly getting fed up with my life. Some times I would reminisce on the opportunity I lost at the Cement Factory. It would put me in a deep state of depression and to begin contemplating suicide again. I had one consolation in that a relative on my grandmother's side, a man named Harvey Babb was the principal of the Tunapuna Government School. My mother took me to see him at his home in Woodbrook. He was a bachelor and he became my counselor. I did odd jobs for him and he in turn helped me to improve on my reading and arithmetic.

He was a very quiet man. I had great respect for him. I had no friends; my mother was the only person I could go to with the exception of Br George Bowen. I was entertaining a lot of suicidal thoughts at this time in my life because nothing positive was happening to me. That was about to change.

I saw an ad in the newspaper The Trinidad and Tobago Hotel and Catering School was looking for young men and women to train to become waiters and waitresses. I told myself: this is what I wanted to do. So I went down to the John Donaldson Technical Institute on Wrightson Road and got the application references that were needed. That was the easy part. I got one from my mother's cousin, Harvey Babb, the Principal of the Tunapuna Government School and the other from Br George Bowen.

Applicants were required to have a clean record and this frightened me because I had one mark against me in San Fernando and I didn't believe they would accept me into the school with a criminal record. I discussed the matter with my mother and she told me to put the application in any way. I did and I was accepted into the school sometime in December of 1962 without the document from the police department. The course was to start in January of 1963. I was told the document had to be in my possession on the first day of school. I was scared about whether I would be accepted. The rest is history. Mr.Eroll Lau, Mr. Henry Beckles and a man named Soloman ran things at the school.

Mr. Lau was the principal and I was really happy that I was accepted into the school even though I wanted to leave my country at the time. It was a six-month course with graduation in June of 1963. I was still living at the hostel on Duncan Street, but the acceptance into the school put things in a different perspective for me. I was anxious to start school even though I did not have that important document. My mother on the other hand was having her problems because the Peels were leaving the country and she had to change jobs. She also had to change her boyfriend because she had dumped the guy but he would not accept that. I met him one day at my mother's job arguing with her at the white people's place and I knew the guy and I were going to get into it. If I had a gun on that day, I would have shot him in the mouth for the things he told me my mother did to him. I will never forget his name or what he told me. He had a filthy mouth and I wanted to kill this man. He was short and stocky and I was no match for him physically, but after what he said all my fear for him left me. My mother saw that look in my eyes and she knew I had a bad temper. She took my hand and told me to go and sit in her room but I wanted to murder the creep. I sat in my mother's room listening when my mother told him to leave the place. When I suspected he was gone, I picked up a knife my mom had in her room and bolted out of the Peels yard with the twelve-inch blade in my waist. He did not have a car and I suspected I could catch him before he caught the bus or a taxi.

I started running after him; my mother was calling out to me, but I was focused on catching the slime ball. I did not pay her any mind and my mother later told me that I had fire in my eyes. I caught up with the jerk and pulled the knife from my waist. He had a newspaper in his hand and when he saw the knife, I saw fear in his eyes. I started swinging at him with the blade but he was blocking his face with the newspaper. I was going to kill him. I felt the knife hit metal. It was his watch. Then I saw blood and he started running. It was then I felt arms around me from the back. It was my mother. I remember her saying:

"Boy you crazy or what you are going to get your self in trouble." She took the knife away from me and walked me back to her room at the Peels house. I never saw the creep again and I was glad about that. The Peels left Trinidad and Tobago and my mother stayed at the house in Cascade until all of the Peels things were removed from the house. She later moved to Morvant, a village East of Port of Spain with a man from Tobago named Nat.

CHAPTER 13

HOTEL SCHOOL

I was doing odd jobs around the city, waiting on classes to start at John D. I was still frequenting the hill on Picton road and still going after Curleen but nothing had changed. She still wanted to have nothing to do with me and I didn't know why. I believe that after the word got out that I was caught stealing from Uncle Eversly's store, it killed my chances with her. What this giggly bare footed plumb-eared Trinidadian beauty had on me I didn't know. One thing was for sure: I had eyes only for her.

The course at the hotel school started some time in January of 1963. I was happy about that, but I still did not have that important document from the Criminal Department of the Law Enforcement and that gave me an uneasy feeling. Three weeks into the class, I started to relax because no one asked me for it and I left it at that. Students I became friendly with were Glen Ross, Aileen Maynard, and Germane Alsopp.

Television was being introduced in Trinidad at this time. Glen Ross, Mr. Erroll Lau and I went on TV to demonstrate the right and wrong way to serve a beer; Mr. Lau was the guest at the table, and the beer was a Carib. Glen served the wrong way and I did it the proper way. Whether it was a commercial or not, I don't know. I did not get paid and I don't know if Glen or Mr.Lau did. I hope the tape is still in the archives of the Television Station.

Things were going fairly well for me. We were learning the art of serving and setting of tables. We were also learning about different wines, different types of meats and what wine goes with what meat and the different courses in a dinner party; I learned words like Demitasse, and ala Carte. I also learned about the different plans that hotels worked under and the importance of personal hygiene. I remembered a Dr. Marcano coming in to teach us about that. As a student, I did a lot of cocktail parties throughout the city arranged by the school. Of course, the pay was good and I was mixing with a lot of highly educated and powerful people. Thoughts of leaving Trinidad and Tobago simmered for a while and I was not thinking about any curse, or light, which I thought I had on me. My self-esteem was soaring at this time period in my life. I clean-bowled a West Indies Opening batsman, Conrad Hunt. Cricket was in the air because the Indian cricket team was on tour and they were in Trinidad to play the West Indies in a test match at the Queen's Park Oval. I got into the oval as a helper with a friend

named Nackum who sold soft drinks and lemonade. I
remembered the West Indies had won the toss. They
were batting first. I wandered over to the warm up area
opening batsman for the West Indies. Mr. Conrad Hunt
was warming up with a few other cricketers. The Indian
spin bowler, tall and slim Saleem Durani was bowling to
Mr. Hunt. I moved in and started fielding and throwing
balls back to Saleem and he in turn motioned me to
come up and bowl a few to Mr. Hunt. The very first
ball I clean-bowled Mr. Hunt with an off break. I was
very surprised and I tried to do it again, but Mr. Hunt
got serious. Saleem kept throwing me the ball. I kept
bowling to Mr Hunt until it was time for him to go in to
bat. Was this my fifteen minutes of fame? I don't know.
Through it, all no words were spoken by Saleem Durani
or Mr. Hunt or myself.

I loved Carnival time in Port of Spain. My favorite
band was the Carib Tokyo but I had this special place
in my heart for the Desperadoes "Despers" Steel Band.
To me the highlight of Carnival in the early sixties
was the Steel Band show. It really was, especially
the competition on Park Street at five o'clock in the
morning. I have heard some of the sweetest Pan music
at the corner of Park and Charlotte streets on a Carnival
Monday. Sounds that I will never forget. Much credit
must be given to the makers of the Steel Pan instrument
and also to the tuners, the arrangers, and the players and
the people who believed in and supported the Steel Band
movement. Ms Beryl Mc Burnie, our Prime Minister,
Dr Eric Williams I have to mention here.

CHAPTER 14

GRADUATION TIME

I graduated from the hotel school sometime in June of 1963. We were all filled with joy and a sense of accomplishment. I was happy I made it through the course, flaky, as I was when the course started. I was always aware that I was accustomed to starting something and never finishing, so graduating from the hotel school was a small triumph for me. I wanted to go to the Hilton Hotel to work after graduation but that did not happen. I was sent to Farrell House Hotel to do my internship. The Farrell House Hotel was about twenty-five miles south of Port of Spain and just outside the village of Saint Margaret, on a hill over looking the Gulf of Praia. From that location you could see the Point a Pierre jetty where the huge oil tankers came in to load and off load their cargo at the oil refinery.

The front of the hotel was on the west side and the landscaping was beautiful all around the hotel. About fifteen feet from the front entrance of the hotel the land sloped down toward the sea. The Hotel was about two hundred feet above sea level it and had a great view of the sea line. The McGrath's were British and they were managers of the Farrell House hotel. The hotel was part of a chain and one branch was located on the west side of Port of Spain and there was also a branch in Tobago called the Blue Haven Hotel at Bacolet Point. I don't remember who the Maitre D was at the time, but the waiters were Gandhi Rackal, Bingo, Scope Phillip, and later on a wonderful brother named John who later became my good friend. I must mention the young David Wall, Mr. Harold Mc Nish, and Bingo. I became good friends with them all. Karl Parry was the food and beverage manager. He was about four feet, six inches tall and he was very smart, intelligent and funny.

In the kitchen we had Chef Lewis from Tobago and my popular friend Charlie Brown a good cook and a kind human being. James Bacchus from Tobago was the barman and another brother named Hall was his assistant. We had a good crew at The Farrell House Hotel and I now believe that the Maitre D was a white European foreigner who spoke several languages, but I don't remember his name. I became good at what I was doing at the hotel and so did the other guys. We all had room and board and our Annex was located about one hundred yards from the hotel's main building. On our days off, we played cards together and we partied a little. I was twenty-four years old and I had never even heard of the word marijuana. We all drank a little liquor but we were all drug free and it's good to be able to say that.

I had given up my bed at the Duncan Street Hostel but on my days off I would still go to Port of Spain to shop and sometimes I would go to the hill to play a soccer game. During my visits to the hill, I would still try to capture the heart of the young Curleen Belfast even though she wanted no part of me. I was a big time waiter and making good money at the Farrell House Hotel. I was also dressing very nicely and I thought that she would surely go for me then. I had heard she was seeing some guy, but I was not concerned because young men usually lie about their exploits with women; I had learned that very early in life and so I was not concerned about the rumors.

I had worked about for a year at the Farrell House. The McGraths had left the hotel due to rumors that they were skimming from the top. Harold McNish joined the staff in 1964; he was brought in as Maitre D.

He was a great individual and we became good friends. At Farrell House, we served many world leaders. One such leader was the late Leopold Sengar of Senegal. I remembered he had a short conversation with Bingo and me and after he spoke he shook our hands and then he left. That was a moment I will never forget.

I still had my heart set on Curleen and today, when I look back, I still don't know what I saw in her. I went to Picton Road to visit my cousin Joe. Joe told me that there was a problem with Curleen, which the guy she was going with had tried to force himself on her and she started screaming. Joe said there was police involvement, but at the same time, everyone seemed to be telling different stories about what had happened.

The man name was Gregory and she must have liked the man because they were seeing each other for some time. What happened on this particular day I don't really know but it was obvious he wanted some of her, and she was not giving in or was not ready to give herself up. I suppose this created the whole situation. After that episode, Curleen started to look my way and she appeared to be anxious to start a friendship with me. I had no problem with that but I believe that she didn't really want me. She had wanted the man Gregory and I caught her on the rebound. Gregory had probably gotten tired of taking no for and answer; little did he know that Curleen was still a virgin and little did I know that she was still in love with the guy five years later. She named our second son Wesley Gregory Patrick. The Wesley came from a chance meeting she had with the great West Indian cricketer Wesley Hall and the Gregory from Gregory the looser. Was I sleeping with the enemy? Was this what is called unrequited love? I didn't care because this Trinidadian beauty was mine, but I believe that she didn't really care for me. She only accepted me because of the embarrassment Gregory had caused her.

We started dating in 1964. I wrote her mother for her hand in marriage while I was courting her and we got married in early 1965, the same year we had our first son Chrisostom Merrill Patrick. I am proud to say that Chris is a Gunnery Sergeant in the United States Marines Corp today. Chris's Godfather is an Engineer who is British and who happens to be white. He stayed at the Farrell House and we became friends. Merrill would be proud to see how his Godson turned out.

The year was 1966. I was going on my fourth year at the Farrell House Hotel but things were getting slow around that time. From 1963 to 1966, the hotel had changed at least six managers and the word was they were just incompetent managers. The hotel was loosing money and things were getting shaky. Layoff rumors were in the air. I was married with a wife and son and we had an apartment in Marabella. My mother had moved back to Marabella and she was living with us, plus the fact that my father, of all people, was visiting us on a regular basis and even helping out with the rent and food. I learned that my father did not like my wife. I didn't know why; he never told me that but he mentioned it to my mother who told me how he felt. I didn't say anything to him about it. I was sent to Tobago to work at the Blue Haven Hotel, but little did I know that I was sent there to be fired because if they had laid me off at the Farrell House, they would have had to pay me severance pay and other fringe benefits. The Blue Haven was over a hundred and fifty feet above sea level at the Bacolet Point, which was overlooking the ocean with a beach at the bottom. The hotel was a three-story structure with seventy five to a hundred rooms and pink in color. The dining room and kitchen were separate from the main building and a man named Chris Grundland was the manager. The accountant was an Indian brother from Trinidad and his name was Mohammed.

CHAPTER 15

TOBAGO

The staff at the hotel in Tobago greeted me warmly. The man in charge of the dinning room was a man named Bishop and he was from Barbados. Then there was Leslie Saul who took over when Mr. Bishop was not around. Leslie and I became good friends; I just don't remember the names of the other waiters. I remember a man named Wiley who was the bartender. In the kitchen there was a man I will never forget because of his love and kindness towards me. Durbin Crooks was about six feet four inches tall; he was the Chef and he was the friend of almost everyone at the hotel. He was a big, Black man and very friendly. I grew to like him more than any other man I have met; we became very good friends and when my wife came to Tobago to spend time with me, Durbin gave us his room so that we could have some quiet time between us. Everyone was nice to us. The head-house-keeper was another person I will never forget even though I don't remember her name. There was another outstanding individual at the Blue Haven who was the world famous Calypsonian, Orthnell Bacchus better known as the Crusoe Kidd. I loved it in Tobago and I really enjoyed the beautiful white sandy beaches with its clean clear waters, the amazing Buccoo Reef and my favorite spot Fort George. On a clear day you can see Trinidad from Fort George in Tobago.

Tobago is located northeast of Trinidad. At first I was stunned by the hospitality of the people I met and worked with in Tobago. I believe that it was mainly because of the preconceived notions I had about the people of Tobago that was based largely on the negative propaganda that was placed in my mind at a very early age. Since I was a little boy I always heard Trinidadians speak negatively about Tobagonians, but during my stay in Tobago I grew to realize that they were wrong. I got my driver's license in Tobago. I was introduced to and ate most of the island's delicious foods including curried pelican and dumplings. In Tobago, the people really made me feel very important. During my time at the hotel, I was privileged to meet in the dining room the British actor John Mills and his wife and their daughter world famous actor Haley Mills. I was their personal waiter for many of their meals and I had many conversations with them. I was making money but at the same time the tips and gratuities were put on the check and the waiters never got their fair share.

Once again rumors of skimming were in the air at the hotel. The accountants Grundland and Mohammed were prime suspects; I didn't like Grundland because

I felt he was ripping off the hard working people at the Hotel who were all black people with no recourse and they took what was given to them without complaint. The Hotel was making money but at the end of the month when I saw what I got in my pay packet I was frustrated as hell. It was only the love of the people that kept me calm, and helped me to enjoy my stay in Tobago. My wife Curleen returned to Trinidad after staying with me in Tobago. I will never forget one of the nights we went out with a few of the hotel's guests whom I became friendly with. We went to another hotel where there was a big party in progress. Our Boys Steel Band was playing that night and my wife and I started to dance. We soon became the main focus of the other dancers in the party and suddenly the people formed a ring around us and we were the only couple dancing and everyone was clapping and laughing: it was really a wonderful experience. I was a very loyal husband and happy in my marriage and although there were many temptations I resisted them all.

This beautiful little Island of Tobago stole my heart, but it was only because of the warmth of the natives and their love and hospitality which eventually captured my heart. I took part in a talent show at one of the local nightclubs and I came in amongst the eventual winners. I came in second to a local kid named Philmore King. I don't remember the song I sang but for the second prize I received a beautiful tea set. Philmore was great and I thought the kid had a lot of potential, but what he did with it, I don't know.

As for me, my life at this point was really great. I was not thinking of any curse, or any light on my head or any bad luck. I was feeling good about myself and my self-esteem was at an all-time high. Tobago was the place for me. I started entertaining thoughts of getting a piece of land in Speyside, which was East Tobago because I heard I had some relatives there. This really got me excited whenever I thought of it, but all those thoughts were laid to rest when Grundland fired me from my job at the hotel. I was really shocked, angry and hurt when it happened. I was working the breakfast shift and I took an order for a table of four. When I brought the food to the table, one of the guests changed his mind and I had to take his plate back to the kitchen. I will never forget the order: scrambled eggs, bacon and toast. I took the order back to the pantry and I thought that this order was going to be my breakfast. I decided that as soon as my shift was over I was going to have that meal. Sure enough, as I was eating in the staff break-room, Mr. Grundland came in and saw me eating the food. He asked me where I got the food and I explained the circumstances to him. He didn't care about that and he told me I was fired. I couldn't believe it...everyone was in doubt. I was mad and I wanted to punch him in his face because I felt in my heart that he should not fire me for that. I would not fire a waiter for something like that. It was a crushing blow and I had no recourse. My co-workers were all surprised at my dismissal and they were all sad to see me leave, but there was nothing they could do about it. I left Tobago sad, depressed and dejected.

When I got to the Farrell Hotel in Trinidad they told me there was nothing they could do. I was convinced then, that it was all a setup.

I went to the John Donaldson Hotel School to see if they could help or even find me another job: they told me to keep in touch; they would try to help me. I did find some work at the In and Out Restaurant on Frederick Street Port of Spain owned by Mr. Lau but it was only part time. I had a wife and son to take care of and things were getting rough. I had to quit the job at the In and Out because of the traveling expenses. I could not afford to pay to come to work on my part time salary.

1967 was a rough year my family and I in Marabella. I give thanks to my mother and father for their help and support at that time. My wife and I had no income but we did make it through the rough times with my parents' help. Thoughts of a curse and a light started to take hold of me once again. Thoughts of leaving Trinidad and Tobago also became much stronger.

Late November of 1967, I paid the hotel school a visit and I received some fantastic news. A man named Jaime Garcia was coming to Trinidad from St Croix US Virgin Islands to hire waiters and waitresses to work at the Estate Carlton Hotel and Golf Course. The only problem was the school had already submitted the names of the potential workers and on top of that, I did not have a passport or money to travel if I got selected. Those selected were given a plane ticket and they would be given room and board with good wages. Even though my name was not on the list, I was told that I could get a job if I made my way there.

CHAPTER 16

ST CROIX, US VIRGIN ISLAND

Mr. Lau had told me if I could get there I was sure to be hired. I got my passport in January of 1968 with the help of my mother and father. I left Trinidad and Tobago on January 28th for the US Virgin Island, St Croix.

It was late afternoon when we landed on Cruzan soil. Hamilton Airport, located on the outskirts of Fredericksted, looked quiet and friendly and compared favorably to Piarco, Barbados, and Antigua airports where the plane made stops on our way to our intended destination. The immigration and custom processes were easy and I was allowed into the island. The trip from the airport to the Estate Carlton Hotel was easy and short. The cab fare was reasonable and I was happy about that because I only had a few dollars in my pocket.

I was very concerned and apprehensive about my situation. I had left my wife and son back in Trinidad. With little or no money in hand I had to make it here...it was Hollywood or bust. The hotel was about a quarter mile from the main road on the southwestern side of the island and was located on sprawling grounds covered with greens and trees, all on flat land. On the other side was the seaside of the hotel and in the middle, it had a Spanish flavor, which reminded me of the movie Zorro. The main building housed the front desk and the main dining room. Breakfast was served on the outside around the swimming pool and the area was partially covered. With suitcase in hand, I went to the front desk to see Mr. Garcia who was out at the time. A Trinidadian named Bobby Wills was at the front desk along with another Trini named Cardinez who had a brother working in the dining room. I felt good about meeting my homies on my arrival at the hotel. It helped me to relax a bit. I was sent to the dining room area. It was around five or six in the evening

I was looking for the Maitre D, a man named Peter Renz who was European. The waiters were all very busy setting up for dinner and no one knew where Mr. Renz was at the time. I sat and waited for a while and a waitress named Mary who was at the bar preparing for a cocktail party came over to where I was seated. We had a brief conversation and I went back to continue waiting for Mr. Renz. Later on a Mr. Garcia came and I introduced myself to him. He welcomed me to St Croix and said he was expecting me. Mr. Lau had told me that he was going to call Mr. Garcia and tell him I was coming. He did and I felt good about that. Mr. Garcia took me to where I was going to be staying at the staff housing, which was about a quarter of a mile from the main building. There were six of us in a twenty-four by twenty-four room. There was one bathroom in the building and three double-decked beds in the room. All the waiters in the room were Trinidadian, but there were other buildings close to ours and similar in design which housed brothers from Antigua, St. Lucia, Dominica, St Kitts, and Nevis. I was introduced to some of the guys who were there and the others I met later. It was the first time I had traveled outside the country of my birth and the island didn't seem to be much different from Trinidad. The ambiance was about the same. It was basically a tropical environment with lots of sunshine, beautiful beaches, nice hotels and a lot of white people from different parts of the world; some of whom owned property on the island and others who came on vacation. I learned this from my research on the US Virgin. The next day I had to go to personnel to fill out the application forms and to get my immigrant status in order. I had come in on a seventeen day visa but I had to get work papers, which meant I had to travel to the British Virgin Island of Tortola for what they called bonding and this had to be done before my seventeen days visa expired. I had to get my passport stamped at the British Customs then come back to St Croix where I was given a six month work visa which had to be extended at a later date. I arrived on a Saturday and I started working on a Tuesday. Monday was orientation and I met with Peter Renz on the day I started work. Homeboys were Howie, Huntley, Mr. Freddy Taylor, Arnold Yow Foo

Cardinez, Capt. Phillip and a few others whose names I have forgotten. Mr. Taylor who later became Maitre D was a man I learned a lot from. I don't believe he had a college education, but he was a quality individual.

In a few months I was into the main stream of things; I met a lot of wonderful people at the hotel and made a lot of friends and contacts from America. Most of the kitchen staff was European. We all got along but it was obvious that they were better paid and better treated than we were. In terms of housing they were situated two to a room, whereas, in the same size room, there were six of us. They also ate better than we did. That did not last very long because we all got together as Trinidadians and signed a petition for better housing and better food. We did get some changes, but basically things stayed the same. Credit must be given to Lawrence Huntley, Alexander Howie, and Mr. Freddy Taylor for the leadership and courage they showed in working for better working conditions at the hotel. I made dining room captain in about six Months, and had my own station.

I was doing very well. I became friendly with Mr. Norman Rockwell, the world famous artist. He and his wife were guests at the hotel at the time and they always wanted to eat in my station. This made me feel very good about myself. I had lots of photographs of Mr. Rockwell, his wife and myself, which I have lost in my travels.

I had missed my wife and son very much and was looking forward to having them with me. I was getting home sick and I kept asking myself if I made the right decision in accepting the job. On the other side of the hotel industry the construction industry was booming as well. Hess Oil refinery was under construction and the main source of the work force was from Trinidad and Tobago. It was a great boost to the economy of the Virgin Islands and still the people seemed to be less friendly towards people from the island that came to work. I did not understand why this was so. It was a real culture shock to me. Some came up in our faces and called us aliens and told us that we should go home to our own countries. The animosity was everywhere. The politicians were using the situation to get votes but more dangerously, they were fanning the flames of hate. Whether they knew it or not they just did not seem to care. One particular politician who owned a radio station, a man named G Luz James called on the aliens to go back home on a daily basis. I despised the man then; but some twenty-five years later, the same man gave me a job on his radio station as a Disc Jockey from twelve midnight to six: in the morning.

I closed my show with two hours of Gospel Music, thanks to Mrs.Leah Padilla for hooking me up. Mr. James later told me he was a friend of our Prime Minister, Dr. Eric Williams. I worked the station for almost nine months. This was 1994; it was a great experience for me. I eventually saved enough money to bring my wife and my son Chris to be with me in St Croix. It meant making a few trips to Trinidad to go to the US Embassy to get immigration papers in order. We were all going to become US citizens. This was a marvelous thing for the Patrick family. With my wife and son with me, I was more comfortable and happy with my life. My brothers, Tony and Dennis, also made the trip to

St Croix, with our mother close behind. Tony worked for Litwin Construction Firm at Hess Oil Refinery as a pipe fitter, and Dennis in the hotel industry. He did not stay there very long.

My second child, a son also, was born on 5th May 1969. He was a Cruzan, meaning he was born under the American flag, which made him a United States citizen. I was proud of that. We named him Wesley Gregory Patrick. His first two names were my wife's suggestion. The name Gregory I would have objected had I remembered the incident my wife had with this guy, four years ago. Wesley, of course, is the name of the West Indian fast bowler and I had no objection to that, but what was her motivation for naming our son Gregory? I could not understand that.

Business was booming at this time in the US Virgin Islands. It was boosting the economy, which strengthened the tax base and put a little money in everyone's pocket. I was thinking about the curse I thought I had on me, and as a matter of fact. I thought I had beaten it. Things were going well for my family and me. I had a wife and two lovely boys and we were bonding. I was a loyal husband at the time and I trusted my wife with my life. No curse would get me now. The indigenous Cruzan people were beginning to open up to the so-called aliens, and life was becoming much easier for us. Entertainers from Trinidad and Tobago were coming to St Croix on a regular basis Gemini Brass, The Mighty Sparrow, and Lord Kitchener are names I remember. They performed both in Christiansted and Fredericksted. James Brown was a big hit to me.

But St Croix was just a rest stop for most of the citizens of Trinidad. Some would stay for a week or two and the next thing you hear about that person is that they were in New York City; some legally others not so legal. Shopping was great in the Virgin Islands. Liquor and beer were cheap: clothing was inexpensive and the tourist trade was lucrative. Everyone was having a ball.

1970 was both a good and a bad year for the island. Good for me in the sense that my wife and first child, Chrisostom Merrill Patrick became a legal resident alien, in other words, we got our Green Cards. There was much joy in the family. But it was bad for the island because of the Fountain Valley Incident which literally killed the tourist Trade.

What would have happened to the economy of the island if the Hess Oil Refinery was not under construction no, one can say, but it sure saved the day for the US Virgin Islands, a place I fell in love with. 1970 was a year that also had me changing jobs; I was offered a position as assistant Maitr'e D at the Queens Quarters Hotel, a position I gladly accepted. I was the assistant to Jean Perrigore, a Haitian immigrant. Everyone called him Johnny and he called me the infamous Captain Patrick. Johnny was a showman and the hotel guests loved him. He was the most charismatic person I have ever met.

The hotel closed sometime in 1970 and I was out of work again with a wife and two children. I had to find work in a hurry so I decided to sell cars. I found work with Sam Perry Motors as a car salesman. A Trinidadian Calypsonian named Skipper was manager.

We sold Toyotas, but business was very slow and I was laid off after a few months. I got another job right down the street, at the Sutherland Motors car dealership but that did not last very long either. I was beginning to get worried about my situation with a wife and two children: things were getting rough but we had love and that kept us together.

CHAPTER 17

CONSTRUCTION WORKER

There was nothing happening in the hotel industry so there was only one place to turn. I decided to get involved in construction work at the Hess Oil Refinery. I knew some of the guys down there. I had no experience in construction work, but I consider myself a fast learner and I decided I was going to become a welder. I did not know how I was going to make it happen.

There was and open call at the Litwin Construction Firm. I went down and I got hired. This was some time in 1970. Things were beginning to look bright again for my family and me. I had stopped gambling; I had never smoked or drank liquor. I loved playing soccer, which was what I did in my spare time.

I was sent to the Hess shop to work under a man named Vernon Taylor. Some say he was one of the best in the business but the name Lune Alexander kept coming up amongst the names of the other Trinidadians that were crack shots in the field. Lune was my classmate at Mon Repos RC School.

I was in the process of learning a new kind of math, pipe math. The shop had welders like Chadband, Old Man Tex, and Mike Kowlessar who is one of the best welders I have ever seen. There was also a man named HMS Staples who was a very kind and wonderful Jamaican immigrant. There was a Bajan welder there also and other pipe fitters in the crew. They all did quality work. I wanted to become a welder; I believed that I had come to the right place, because those guys were very good. Although I had a wife and two sons, I was still not thinking too much about the future. I was not making any plans. I suppose it was because I didn't know how to really make serious plans. I later learned that, "the man who fails to plan, plans to fail"

My sons were growing nicely, and my thoughts were of taking them to the big USA. As far as the job was concerned, I was making progress. I learned the welding machine, its functions, the different settings, I also learned about pipefittings, the different take off for different pipe sizes, but my focus was on welding. For six months, I used my lunchtime to practice; I was also getting a lot of tips and encouragement from my co-workers, all except one, the man they called Tex. I had my own hood, and when I had the free time, I would put it on and look at the different welders when they worked. I was studying their technique. I was studying Tex's technique one day, and he suspected I was behind him. He stopped welding, took his helmet off, turned around and told me when he was welding not to stand behind him again. I was shocked at his response, because the guys who were much better than him didn't seem to mind it when I looked at their work. I did what he told me, but by the middle of 1971, I was ready to take a welding test. I did and passed with flying colors.

It was truly a great feeling. I was just a rookie but I was told I had the potential to become one of the best. I was sent out into the field, and even though I was not doing critical work at the time, I was on my way to becoming a first class welder. My family and myself moved in with a co-worker named Mike and his girl friend, Pam. We got along very well. We had a two-bedroom apartment and we had enough money saved for my wife and kids to take a vacation, which they did.

I got laid of shortly after my family went on vacation, but I had enough welding hours under my belt to secure a job with the Fisher- Hess Company. The company was dredging the harbor at the south end of the refinery, and a wonderful Trinidadian guy nicknamed 'Episode' was my foreman. We were working on the dredge and I was one of the welders. Episode taught me a lot while I was under his supervision and today I am in a position where I can teach others. I got laid off from the Fisher-Hess job, and got re- hired with Litwin Construction Company all in early 1972.

There was a new phase in the expansion work at the refinery, and it meant another two years of work without any chance of being laid off. My brothers, Tony and Dennis, and my mother had already left for the United States of America. Tony went to New York, and Dennis to Ohio. My mother went to New Jersey to work for the Vorbach family, a family I became friendly with while working at the Hotel Queens Quarters. My brother Tony wrote me from the US and told me about his membership into the Steam Fitters Union 638. He told me it was one of the most powerful unions in the world and he also sent me an application form to apply. Minorities were usually barred from becoming members of this particular trade union; my brother told me Mayor Lindsay was very helpful in opening the doors for minority membership. He also said there was strong resistance against it by the old membership. This stimulated my interest, and I wanted to become a member of the union because of the wages. It was by far the best in the world and I wanted to be part of it. That did not happen until 1974.

CHAPTER 18

MY WORST EMBARRASSMENT

I was alone again and then the curse just seemed to have caught up with me again. Mike, his girl and I were getting along fine, but I had suspected she was disloyal to Mike with a local boy. I never said anything to him about it. She was very nice to me, and like a fool, I misread her behavior for something else. I thought she was flirting, but it was just brotherly love that she had for me. I took a day off one day to find out. Mike was at work on this day, and I was in my room plotting on how to approach her. I finally made up my mind to call her into my room to rub my shoulders for me. I was sitting on the edge of my bed. She came and sat next to me and started rubbing my shoulders. I turned and put my arm around her and she pushed me away and ran out the room screaming. At that point I wished the earth would have open up and sucked me in. I was ashamed of myself. I started, calling myself a fraud, a hypocrite, and a phony. I sat in my room for hours. I was in shock. Little or nothing happened, but it was enough to make me want to kill myself.

How would I explain my actions to Mike? He was a cool guy, but how would I explain my actions to my wife and children? Up to this day I don't remember what explanation I gave to Mike, but I was very apologetic. I am sure those who heard about the incident started looking at me differently. I was also beginning to wonder what kind of a person I was. I didn't have any college degrees, but I was filled with knowledge. How could I make such a serious error in judgment? Nevertheless I had to go on with my life. I also had to move out of the apartment. The embarrassment was too much to bear and I could not face Mike or his girl. I was out of the apartment in two weeks. I moved into a new housing complex in the Grove place area just behind the newly built Isaac Hayes apartments. Several Trinidadian brothers made their homes there as well. Ours was a two-bedroom apartment on the ground floor of a three-story villa. It was moderately furnished but we were comfortable. My wife was expecting our third child so we had to save money for the baby's arrival. It was a girl and we named her Kurleen Lillian Patrick. She was given her mother's and grandmother's first name. She is also my first and only daughter.

My family was growing nicely but still I was not doing any planning on a major scale. I was consumed by the thought of taking my family to the United States. I was making progress as a welder at the Hess Oil

Refinery and I was getting better and better as the weeks and months went by. My social life was all about my family. We didn't have many friends except Leon and Bernice Charles who stayed with us for a short while. A soccer club was formed, in our community, as well as an All Fours Club, of which I was made President; it was the St Croix, St Thomas Alliance. I will never forget the All Fours match where Sam Bull George got angry picked up some of the prizes and smashed them to the ground. It was a wicked act and if I could I would have kicked his ass but he was the big and bad Sam Bull and no one challenged him. Why should I?

1972 came and went,:1973 met me with more confidence in my welding skills and I felt that I was ready to challenge the global community. Because of a white supervisor named John Landry, I was introduced to Tig Welding. John had put me to work with one of the best welders in the business, a guy named Hollis 'Shadow' Murray. I was learning a lot from Murray and he didn't seem to mind. I was truly grateful to him for his kindness. Because of Hollis' help I went on to become one of the best in this field. I was truly disturbed when I heard about the incident between Beef Hacket and John Landry. John Landry seemed like a good person, and I couldn't understand why anyone would try to hurt him.

CHAPTER 19

THE BIGGEST MISTAKE
OF MY LIFE

It was May of 1973. I was ready to move on. I had filled out the application my brother Tony had sent me for membership into the Steam Fitters Union of New York City Local 638.

The mentality I had at the time was that I was the man of the house and I made all the serious decisions. There was little discussion between my wife, my children and myself about us leaving the US Virgin Islands. I felt that my growth and development in St Croix was limited, and it was time to move on.

My mother and two brothers, Tony and Dennis, were already on the mainland in the USA and I wanted my children to bond with their grandmother, so I felt the time had come to move on. I was leaving a job behind with the Litwin Construction Company. Most importantly I was leaving my wife and three children behind, for what I perceived as a better opportunity to expand and to grow; but was I only thinking about myself? I was set to go and I believe I could not fail because there was work everywhere for welders and I figured in six weeks time I would work and save enough money to send for my family. My kids would get a good education in the United States and after a few years, we could all go back to Trinidad and tell about my American experience. We could then kick back and relax in the place of my birth. However; it didn't happen that way. Every thing was set, my brother Dennis would pick me up in Dayton, Ohio, and we would travel to Michigan, which was his base. He had word that a company in Harlingen, Texas was hiring welders. It was a cool winter's night when the plane landed at the Dayton Airport. My brother was late in picking me up, which had me a bit worried. We had a brief conversation; how was my trip, he asked, and I told him it was ok. I mentioned how cool the weather was and the fact that I was just wearing a T-shirt and a jean jacket. He told me it gets really cool at nighttime. It was the first time I'd ever experienced a sixty-degree temperature. We slept in Dayton that night and hit the road for Michigan the next morning. The trip took a few hours and I was truly impressed with the roadways, the great landmass, and the huge farms. I saw all black cows for the first time, State Troopers, deer and everything in abundance, or so it seemed.

I was truly impressed with the scenery on the trip from Ohio to Benton Harbor, Michigan, but this was the United States of America and there was much more to come. We arrived safely, and I was introduced to my sister-in-law, Adele and her daughter. I was asked about my trip, you know, the usual conversation. After a few hours rest, I called St Croix to let my family know that I had arrived safely. I was very anxious, and apprehensive about the move I had made, but I was not afraid because things were opening up for Blacks in the country at this point in time in the areas of jobs, education, housing, and bank loans. As for me, I knew I had a skill that I could take with me any part of the world. I was a welder.

We left Michigan for Houston, Texas, two days after my arrival. We took off in the good car. My brother had a 1971 Monte Carlo. It was a nice car. We came over from Ohio in the Chevy Impala, which I believe it was a 1966 model. The Monte Carlo was a really nice running car. After several hours on the road, we arrived safely in Houston Texas at the house of Adele's sister. The next day we went further south to Brownsville, Texas, where we met Frank Patterson, Felix Marga and a few other brothers from Trinidad. Some were welders, others were pipe fitters, and they were working at a pipe shop not far from where they lived. My sister-in-law, Adele did not make the trip to Brownsville. We stayed in Brownsville for a day then we headed back north to Harlingen, Texas. Word was that a Plumbers Union in Harlingen was looking for welders to send to Richmond, Virginia, and Wichita, Kansas. Sure enough the word was correct and we hit the hall the next morning to sign up to go to Kansas. The union hall was very crowded, but my brother Dennis and I got a referral for the Virginia job. There were quite a few Trinidad welders in the hall that morning. Frank Patterson was there and he too was sent to Richmond. Frank went on to Richmond. My brother Dennis and I went on to Houston to pick up my sister-in-law and from there we headed back to Michigan to drop her off.

We changed cars when we got back. Dennis left the good car with his wife Adele and we came back to Virginia with the Chevy Impala. We did a lot of driving but I was not tired. I was more apprehensive about the future and I was very concerned about my family back in St Croix. The Union Hall was on Broad Street in Richmond at the time. The hall was buzzing with activity when we arrived. It was filled with white workers who gave us very strange looks. Black welders in these parts was not a common sight, but we weren't intimidated: we turned in our referrals. My brother and I were sent to the North Anna Nuclear Plant, which was in Louisa County, about forty miles West of Richmond, just outside a small town named Gordonsville.

The plant was in the boondocks, away from everything. It was huge, and giant cranes were erected around the plant. Workers were busy at their craft and concrete trucks were coming and going. I saw this huge dome built out of steel and concrete and it gave me rush. Was I going to be part of all this? I most certainly hoped so. All I had to do was pass the welding test.

We pulled into the parking lot, got directions from the security guard, got to the lunchroom where the Shop Steward met us and he signed us up. Then he took us to the Test Shop to meet the shop supervisor. In those days, you didn't have to take a drug test. Coming in we heard a lot about Virginia white people and their mentality and attitude towards Blacks but we were not afraid; we came to work. Surprisingly there were other Trinidadian welders in the test booth including HomeBoy Frank Patterson. There was another brother named Charley; he came down from New York. The shop foreman was a white man named Jim. He had worked in Trinidad with a company named Foster Wheeler so he knew that welders coming from Trinidad were supposed to be good. He said so himself, and when he started talking about Roti, and Callaloo, it removed a lot of the pressure and stress I was feeling about the welding test.

The test was your standard pipe test; a six-inch schedule 80 coupons in the six G position and it was going to be x-rayed. Then there were the ten-inch schedule 120 heavy wall coupon tests that was a killer. Both tests took me two days to complete. I passed both tests, but my brother Dennis failed the test, which meant that he had to go back to Michigan, leaving me without any means of transportation. Frank Patterson thankfully took me to and from work. He even gave me his car to get to work one day when he was not feeling well and could not work.

When we got back to Richmond after the first day in the test booth, we rented a room in a hotel in the downtown area. I didn't have much money so it was up to my brother Dennis and his friend who we met on the job to pay the hotel bill. There was a lot of confusion when we got back to the hotel on the second day. My brothers' friend failed the test as well and they left the job early. It was arranged that I would ride back to Richmond with Frank Patterson but something happened that warranted law enforcement intervention.

Dennis and his friend had already left the hotel; Dennis went to Michigan and his friend, I don't know where. When I got to my hotel room it was locked, and I had to go to the front desk to get into my room, and that was when they called the police again. Luckily, Frank Patterson didn't leave in a hurry and when the police came I was given a citation for what I don't know what, but I had to appear in court to answer the charge. I believe it was for non-payment of the hotel bill. I don't really remember but I remember thinking that this was my first day and week in America and I was already in the files of the American justice system. Bummer! When I left Trinidad I thought I had dodged the curse, but here it was again. Was this the beginning of a bright future for me in the United States or was it the start of events that would eventually bring me pain and misery?

In spite of the problems I inherited at the hotel, there was still satisfaction, a sense of accomplishment and great joy after passing the welding test because it meant that I could set plans in motion to bring my family to America. It also meant that I could buy a car and get an apartment or buy a house. I was making considerably more money on this job than when I was working for Litwin Construction at the Hess Oil refinery in St Croix. In addition, affirmative action was the new concept open to Blacks in America, which meant opportunities in almost every facet of life in the country. I came to America at the right time and success or failure was in my hands. After spending about four days in the test booth I was sent out in the field to join a work crew. I was teamed up with a white fitter, but I was happy to know that I was in the same crew as Rivers, a crackshot welder from Trinidad. He was clean. He traveled with a white welder named Frank Trampus. Frank was European but he was just as good as Rivers. Also in the crew were Lewis Lawson and his buddy, Hank. Lewis was the welder, and Hank the fitter. The two men were very helpful to me in adjusting to the American work ethic. I was a speedy welder, and they basically told me not to work so fast. It was an adjustment that frustrated me for a while because I was just coming off a job where I was making six to eight welds a day and on that job if you made two welds a day you were lucky. I had to make that adjustment fast and I did with the help of Frank Patterson.

I found a room in Gordonsville where the rent was cheap and the room was clean. It was there that I met an African American brother named Wesley Watkins. He was a welder from Virginia Beach. The brother was very helpful to me and we became good friends. We worked in the same area and we had lunch together everyday. Wesley was schooling me in the ways of the whites on the job and the Blacks as well but I felt that I could get along with people of any race or color having worked in the hotel industry for ten years. All the laborers on the job were American Blacks. As welders, we were in a higher income bracket. I don't know if that was the reason they never wanted to speak with us. They spoke with Wesley, but they stayed away from the guys from the islands. They were very suspicious of us. We tried to speak to our American brothers but they never encouraged any conversation with us. This truly baffled me because I knew we were the same people.

The women on the other hand were quite hospitable. I soon discovered that Virginia had a large number of Red Bones and I seem to have developed a love for Red Bone women up to this day. As a matter of fact, I am married to one right now and you will discover that as you read.

As the weeks went by I adapted to the American way of life. Work hard for what you want, and you will get it, they say. But truly not everyone believed that. The estimated time of completion of the plant was three to four years and that was for each reactor. I was lucky, and blessed to be where I was. I figured in six weeks, my family would join me in America. After a month in the country, I got my driver's license, and then I bought a car. It was a 1963 Pontiac Lemans. I was very proud of myself. A Virginia DL and my own car in America? Wow. I was doing well on the job. I got a lot of compliments from my co-workers and welding inspectors alike. I was really proud of myself.

I will never forget the morning we had a safety meeting and the foreman of our crew gave me the safety topic to read. After I was done reading every one started applauding. I didn't know why, maybe they thought I couldn't read: they kidded me about my accent. I was saying sweet drink, instead of soda. I was saying sweet soap, instead of bath soap. My pronunciation of some of the words was completely different to theirs, so maybe they decided to check my reading skills. I also remember while working at the Hess Refinery some of the guys called me the English man.

I had good credit, but still I didn't know at the time how important it was to maintain it. I was a person who at the time took everything and everyone for granted. I am extremely happy today to say I am not that way any more. By the way I did go to court to face the charge for the hotel bill, I was happy when the judge threw the case out. I was settling down nicely in Virginia. I had opened a Savings account, and things were looking good for me at this time. I was going to make it in America, or so I thought. I started dating. She was a Red Bone and she told me she loved my accent, which was all she wrote and that was when the lies started to fly. Actually it was one lie, that I was not married. I was denying my wife and children. The calls and letters to St Croix were getting few and far in between. I had practically deserted my wife and children; I would have to pay dearly for this action later.

In my third month in the United States, I bought a brand new Buick Regal. It was tan with a brown top. It was a beautiful car and I was really proud of myself. I felt there was nobody else in the world that could stop me from getting what I wanted or do what I wanted to do. I had forgotten that while I was enjoying myself, my family was struggling to survive in St Croix. It was like I was a totally different person. All the plans I made before I left the Virgin Islands went through the window.

With my new car, I went to New York almost every weekend and every time; I had a chick at my side. I had no difficulty in finding a date. On one of my trips to the Big Apple, I learned that the Salem New Jersey Nuclear Plant was a hiring welder and that was all she wrote. I started making plans for Salem.

In the meantime, my brother Tony and my mother had purchased a home in Asbury Park, New Jersey. My mom had quit her job with the Vorbach family for personal reasons and she started working at a nearby nursing home. This was very encouraging to me and it also motivated me in more ways than one. Four months in America and I had sufficient money in hand to bring my family to be with me but because of the lie I told about not being married, I was starting to believe the lie and I was living it. I started going steady with one of my dates and things were getting serious, very serious. It was time to leave Virginia. I called Local 121 about the job in Salem and they told me to come on down. I left Gordonsville, Virginia in the middle of the night and I haven't been back there since. I was almost six months in the United States and I had saved about fifteen hundred dollars, but still I was not thinking about the predicament my family was in. I had become selfish and self-centered. Was I always like this?

I had considered myself a kind and generous person; how could I do this to my family and what was my motivation? As a young boy growing up in Mon Repos, my aunts told me constantly that I was worthless, that I had a light on me, light meaning Obeah, but look at me now: I was going to show them who was worthless.

CHAPTER 20

NEW JERSEY BOUND

I remembered it was a Monday when I got to the Union Hall in Atlantic City. Local 121 today has merged with Local 322. I had gotten a referral from the Harlingen Local, which was accepted by Local 121. I had submitted my application to Local 638 through my brother Tony and was waiting on a call from them. I had given them my mothers' home phone number for the call. I was determined to become a member of one of the most powerful unions in the world: I was also told it was one of the most racist organizations in the country.

I think I didn't believe it because my brother Tony was a member. I knew there was a lot of resistance towards minority membership in the local unions, but once again, thanks to Mayor John Lindsay for helping to open the door for Blacks and Latinos to become members of this very powerful union. I felt that my background in the hospitality industry would help me to survive whatever I was confronted with and besides that I knew that all whites were not the same. I have hundreds of stories in my portfolio about the white people that had helped me so I was not intimidated. Salem, New Jersey was a small town and mostly Blacks lived there. The main street also separated the Blacks from the whites. I found myself a room in a house on Union Street. I was given a room on the upstairs floor and my room was at the back of the house. I was a bit tired and decided to go in to work on Tuesday morning fresh and rested to take the welding test.

It was close to the winter and this was my first experience of that kind of weather in the country and I was prepared for it. After a good night's rest, I was ready to report to work and do the test. I learned the drill from the Virginia job, go through security, which was not as rigid as it is today, then go find the Union Shop steward and he would sign you up. Then you went to the safety meeting, and on to the test shop. I was sharp, I was confident and I breezed through the test. On the North Anna Nuclear Plant, I had a lot of practice at tig welding, plus I learned a lot from Mike Rivers and Frank Trampus, two of the best in the business. My six-inch stainless steel, schedule 80 coupon test was a masterpiece. I was given a lot of compliments for it. But greater than that was the friendship I developed with a young white welder by the name of Randy Poole. I felt there was something highly spiritual about our meeting; Randy was a good welder with lots of potential but he had little experience in Tig Welding. I showed him the little I knew and he picked that up fast enough to pass the Welding Test. He gave me the credit, but he had done the work.

Out in the field, I met Trinidadian welders who were members of the Steam Fitters Local 638 in New York City and from the Baltimore Local 392, which was just south of Salem. I was surprised to meet Tarzan. He went with my mom when we were living in Marabella, and he was out of the Baltimore Local. I was also surprised to meet the Incredible Winston Simon, one of the most fearless men I had ever met. He worked for Hess at the refinery in St Croix and he was living in Salem with his family. As for my family, after months of suffering in St Croix, they finally made it to the States without my help. I called my mother one day to find out how things were and it was then I learned that my family was there in New Jersey with her.

At this time, I was strong into the relationship with Hazel and I was still living the lie that I was free, single and unattached. I would pay dearly for that lie. On that weekend, I went up to Asbury Park to meet with my family. I was glad they were in the States but I had no explanation to give them as to why I did not help them in their time of need. I had a situation on my hands and I had to deal with it. How they came and who helped them was not even discussed, but it put things in a different perspective. I had my family with me now and I was a husband and father once again. I had to deal with that.

It was a Friday evening when I got to Ashbury Park filled with anxiety and tension. I had let my family down and they suffered in St Croix because of my self-centeredness: now I had to face them. What would I tell them? I was driving a new car and I had a good job. What was my excuse? I had none whatsoever. Finally we met. I hugged and kiss my wife and children for a long time. My daughter had grown. She was three or four, and my sons Wesley and Chris looked skinny but very healthy. My wife had lost a lot of weight. I was so arrogant in my ways that I didn't feel that I was responsible for their condition. What was I turning into?

I was not doing drugs and I was not a heavy drinker, but what was I becoming? My wife and I talked a little and we even made love in the back seat of my car. It was a little sad when I had to leave to get back to work, but mostly I was thinking about Hazel down in Salem, New Jersey. Back in Salem, I had told no one that my family was in the United States. The lies continued. Two weeks later, I had a big surprise. I was getting to work and was about a quarter of a mile down the road from the parking lot when I saw my brothers' car parked on the side of the road and standing next to the car was my wife with my little daughter in her arms. I was in shock. I pulled to the front of my brother's car. In the drivers' seat was my brother's Tony's girl.

My first thought was: what the hell are they doing here! I was pissed and I went to the car fuming because I was busted. I couldn't take them into Salem. What would I say to my landlady? I wasn't supposed to be married. The next thing to do was send them back to Ashbury Park because I certainly couldn't take them to Salem. If I were caught in the lie I would look like a fraud, which was what I was.

February of 1974, I became a member of the Steam Fitters Local 638 in New York City, thanks to my brother Tony. I was given a welding test and a scaled down pipe fitters test. I passed both. The union book at the time was eight hundred plus dollars, today a union card is over five thousand dollars. I was happy and proud of my self.

I felt there was no one like me in the world. Look where I came from and look where I am now, I kept saying to myself. I remember that they told me I was worthless. Look at me now, with a brand new car and membership in one of the world's most powerful union. However, I believe the accomplishments made me more selfish and self-centered; they would hurt me in the long run.

CHAPTER 21

BOSTON OR BUST

Cambridge Western Avenue was the place where we found an apartment. It was located almost at the corner of Putman and Western Ave. It was a six-family house that was owned by a Bajan citizen. It was in a nice location, but not perfect. We were close to a nightclub and you know what that means in terms of noise and people on the streets at nights. Harvard University was just a stone throw away and that was great. Cambridge was just a short walk away from down town Boston and you could walk across the Charles Street Bridge from Western Avenue to get there. You could also take the train, or you could catch a cab. We had a great location. My father-in-law had also moved to Boston and my wife's best friend was living in a small community just east of Boston so it was ideal for our family. But my motivation was to get my family as far away from Salem, New Jersey as I possibly could.

I kept my job at the Salem Plant, but the traveling was wearing me out. On a Friday evening I would hit the road to Boston. The trip was six to seven hours on a good traffic day. By this time Hazel had her third child, my first son with her. I would have to leave Salem and soon. I never wanted to work in New York City so I had to find work in Boston. I was settling down as a father and husband, family man and beginning to like it. It appeared as though my wife had forgiven me because we never spoke about St Croix. I had suppressed the thoughts and the belief that I had a curse on me because things were going well for me at this time period. My children were enrolled in a Cambridge School, which was close to the apartment, and this was a good thing because the school-bussing situation was getting serious. I was truly surprised at that and I didn't want my children to be bussed to a school were they would be in any danger. My wife got pregnant with our fourth child. She delivered a boy and we named him Abubaka Jaramooji Patrick. He was born on 11th November 1974. My wife said no more children and shortly after that she had her tubes tied. I was going on thirty-five years old and still taking things for granted; especially my wife and children that the Lord had blessed me with. I had a good wife and four beautiful children. I knew my wife didn't love me the way I had loved her, but I had the power to change that and I was really trying, but my ways and my thinking were not those of a man who knew the value of what he had. As a matter of fact, I was as secular as I could be and all this was rubbing off on my children, but I never taught them to hate any one. In the end, I would loose it all because of my ignorance.

I didn't have a formal education and I didn't know the Scriptures, so I was doomed to make bad judgments and serious mistakes all through my life.

My friend Carl Smith was the Godfather of my fourth child Abu, and my wife's girl friend BB was the Godmother. Today Abu is grown and married; a wedding invitation was not extended to me, but I wish my son all the best in his married life. He chose a white bride. I have no objections to that but I know there are consequences in marrying outside of one's race. I was determined to make my marriage work, but I also had to deal with my demons and my insecurities. I was living in my own little world, not thinking that I was ever going to get old. My world came tumbling down when a drunk driver ran a stoplight and smash into the rear panel on the driver side of my car. I was in Cambridge for the weekend, and I took the family to Lynn Mass, to visit my wife's friend BB. It was nighttime and we were on our way back to Cambridge and I took a wrong turn and in trying to get back to the freeway the accident happened. Luckily, my family members were not hurt but we were all in shock. To this very day I don't remember how things turned out with this accident, but thoughts of the curse were beginning to bother me. My beautiful car was not beautiful anymore after the accident. I drove back to Salem, sad and depressed, wondering why this thing happened to me. I just didn't get it that this had to happen. I had too much Karma, as a matter of fact, I was overflowing with it,. I informed the insurance company; they sent out an appraiser, who referred me to a Salem body shop to have the car repaired. I argued with the man about totaling the vehicle but he was set in his decision, which pissed me off. I took the car in when I got off work on Monday afternoon. It was going to take a week to ten days to be repaired, which meant I had to bum rides to and from work, but that was the easy part. The difficulty was in staying in Salem on the weekend without any transportation. It also meant that I couldn't travel to Cambridge to be with my family on the weekend. The car was ready in seven days but there were problems when I picked it up. The shop had let me test-drive the car and I was hearing all kinds of noises. This certainly was not the smooth running Buick Regal I bought only ten months ago. What made it worse was that my friend, who took me to get the car that afternoon, went with me on the test run and after hearing the noise, he suggested that he would get out and stand behind the car while I drove away from him. I drove for less than a hundred yards, then he signaled me to come back and when I got alongside of him, he told me the chassis of the car was bent. That depressed me even more. When we got back to the shop, I discussed the possibility of the bent chassis with the shop owner who said he didn't believe that it was. We had to leave the car behind because I was still waiting on the insurance company to mail me the check for the repairs, which was something they did in those days. The check was made out in my name, a practice that was discontinued in the early seventies for obvious reasons.

When the check came I promptly called the insurance company and told them I didn't want the car and that they could come and pick it up. They already knew where it was. I took the check and I went out and bought a second hand two door 1965 Wildcat. I never heard from the dealer again partly because I had a Virginia address and I was living in Cambridge, Massachusetts. When I moved from Virginia I did not leave a forwarding address. That action was the beginning of the end of my good credit. It was February 1975. I was still working at the Salem Nuclear Plant and the drive back and forth from Cambridge to Salem New Jersey was getting the best of me. I was also a little depressed about the loss of my new car, but the Wildcat was running well so my movements were not restricted. Eventually, I quit the Salem Job. I left Salem in the middle of the night close to a Friday; I had gotten paid on Thursday. I said F--- It to Salem, New Jersey. I couldn't take the double life any more. I was a father, husband and breadwinner in Cambridge, Mass, and a loose and free as a bird person in New Jersey. This was no way to raise a family. I was a very impulsive person, and prone to making impulsive decisions. This was not a very good way to be, especially for a man trying to raise a family.

My family was happy about the move. Now, the objective was to find work as a welder in the Boston area. I felt that would not be difficult. As a matter of fact, I found work the next week at the sugar refinery in Charlestown, which was east of Cambridge and only a short drive away. I was feeling a sense of relief like a weight was lifted off of my shoulders. I was at home with my wife and kids and this meant a lot to me because my children were growing up nicely. I was reconnecting with my first two sons, Chris and Wesley.

Early mornings especially on weekends, we all went jogging around the Charles River. We did two sometimes three laps. Wesley was always lagging behind but Chris always stayed with me and I was truly impressed with that; I am not surprised that Chris is a United States Marine today. He showed me he had that mental toughness and the determination as a little boy.

The free spirit took hold of me again and I was gone again in July 1975. This time I headed out to Benton Harbor, Michigan. The Cook Nuclear Plant was hiring welders and the pay was better than the Sugar Refinery, but I believe the real reason I wanted to go there was because my mother had moved from Asbury Park to Benton Harbor. My brother Dennis was also living with his girl in the same area. After four months in Benton Harbor, I decided to go back to Cambridge, to be with my family

What was really happening in my life at this time, I don't know. Was it somebody or something trying to separate me from my family or was it just my ego and I? I was a damn good welder and wanted to show the world how good I was and I would have gone to any state or any country with my skill. Was that the reason? Maybe it was, or was it because I was told as a little boy that I was worthless, and now I was trying to prove to the world that it wasn't so. How these things work, I don't know but something strange was going on in my life and I didn't know what it was. I got back to Cambridge, spent about a week with my family, and then I was gone again; this time to Canada, just outside of Maine, in a little town called St. John. The company of Babcock and Wilcox was the main contractor at the Irvin Oil Refinery. There was an open call from the Union Hall and I was gone again. My wife didn't say any thing to me. She just went along with the program. When I got into St John it was snowing and there was already two feet of snow on the ground, from a snowstorm that came through the week before. I was asking myself what the hell was I doing here, but I was there already so I told myself that I was going to make it. I passed the welding test and in a months time I was back in Cambridge, leaving behind my friend Trevor Red fig Larode who I had met there on the job. We worked for different foremen at the refinery. I was going through a very difficult period at this time in my life and I didn't have any answers. I trusted no one and I did not take advice from anyone. I was arrogant and I was full of style but I had no substance. I did love my wife and children, but why was I running away from them? I did not have a clue of why I did. I decided to make a greater effort to make my marriage work.

We were into the year 1976. I found work with the Local Pipe Fitters Union in Boston and I was teamed up with two brothers from Trinidad. One of the brother's names was Thaddeus and we worked well together. Then I was laid off because work contracts for the union were slow. Besides, I was a traveler and travelers in the union world get laid off first. That was standard procedure. Between jobs I took a two-week bartenders course at Harvard University, since we lived in walking distance to University. To me, this was a huge accomplishment. I was a Harvard graduate. I had a degree in Mixology and I could go to any part of the world and be a bartender. I walked the hallways of the university where great men had walked. I sat in the auditorium where greater men had sat. Among them was the first Prime Minister of my country Trinidad and Tobago who was a Harvard graduate. It was a boost to my self-esteem. I didn't really need it because I already had a big head, but I did feel really good after graduation that was held in one of the auditoriums on campus. I was planning to find work as a part-time bartender but then I found welding work at the General Dynamics Shipyard in Quincy, Mass. It was a nonunion position and the pay was small compared to union wages, but the main thing was: I was home every evening with my family. My union could have brought me up on charges if they knew I was doing non-union work. I didn't care about that. I gave up my desire to work part time as a bartender because I figured that would take me away from my family, I had taken my family for granted and I had to do every thing in my power to change that. My kids were doing well in school and they needed all the encouragement that they could get. All was going well until the roving spirit began to take hold of me again. I had only worked a few months at the shipyard and had gotten word that there was an open call at the Salem plant. I hated going back to Salem to work because of the manner in which I left. I told no one I was leaving on that night in February. I had to go back because the pay was good and the union had just gotten a pay raise and I wanted some of it. Besides, I had a union book in my pocket and I loved working union, because in nonunion work if you get fired you have no recourse; with the union that was different.

I called the union hall. This was in late November
1976. They were hiring and they told me to come down
the Wednesday of the following week because that was
when they sent out travelers. I told my wife about
the move. I didn't even discuss it with her; I just said
that was what I was going to do. I was shocked when
she told me that if I left, it was over between us: she
was going to get a divorce. With my selfish self, I got
angry. I told her she was jealous of me, that I was the
breadwinner. She couldn't tell me what to do and all the
other nonsense that an idiot like me would say under
these circumstances. In retrospect, I see that I was a
little fool who didn't know what he had. That Monday
I secured a loan from a financial company. My friend,
Carl Smith was my cosigner and on a Tuesday morning
in November 1976, I took off for Salem, New Jersey
with the threat of a divorce hanging over my head.

CHAPTER 22

DIVORCED

I got lucky because Local 121 had merged with Local 322, which meant that I didn't have to go to Atlantic City to answer the job call. I got the job and three weeks later I was back in Cambridge Mass. only to meet with the unexpected. My wife was indeed serious about her threat, and she was really through with me. It devastated me and I was really hurt and I didn't like the thoughts I had running through my mind at that time. I must confess that in my arrogant state I had entertained thoughts of hurting her. I knew that she had called the police, but they said that there was nothing they could do. I was still the father and husband and there was no restraining order. When the police left, I took all four of my children and turned right around and headed back to Salem, New Jersey. I was determined to keep my children. I was dating a woman by the name of Suzie Shorter at the time and she had a small two-bedroom house. She took me in with my four children even though she had two other kids that she had adopted by herself. I did not realize it at the time, but in my haste to leave Cambridge, Mass., I had left all of my children's birth certificates behind and this was going to create a serious problem for me because without those papers I could not register them in school. I also knew that the chance of my wife sending them to me was slim. I was in great jeopardy because of this dilemma, plus the fact that I was in a rather stressed out emotional state.

In looking back, I am sure that my children received the worst of it and would be greatly affected by the entire situation. I realized that as parents, we were not thinking about our children, or I might say that I was not thinking about the effect the situation would have on my children, when I decided to take them away. When parents decide to end a marriage, they just want to get away from each other and the focus is mainly on them and they often do not take into consideration the effects of their actions on the children that are involved. The eventual divorce had an adverse effect on me and I believe it had a greater effect on my children even up to this day. Today, I take the full blame for whatever had transpired between my children's mothers and me during that time.

Hazel, a former friend of mine, had moved out of Salem, NJ with her kids. I learned of this after inquiring about her and was informed that she had moved to another town. I was not able to get any further information about her and I did not know her address. In all honesty, I made no effort to find her and sent no messages that I wanted to see her.

With the state of mind I was in at the time and the situation I was trying to get under control; I felt the best thing to do was to leave Hazel alone. I decided to volunteer my services as a soccer coach for the kids in the neighborhood. Soccer coaching the six to nine year old kids had a lot of therapeutic value for me during that difficult time. I also thought of my ex-wife and my children and even though I blamed myself for what had happened, I was beginning to hate her more and more. I didn't like the thoughts that I was entertaining towards her. I got the coaching position through my friend Byron, whom I consider to be a wonderful person and a good soccer player who just happen to be white. We played many good soccer games together. Byron lived in Bridgetown, which was a half-hour away and east of Salem. His family owned a sporting goods store in Salem and Byron was store manager. I bought my first two sons their bicycles at Byron's store, and a friendship developed between Byron and me. Through our friendship, Byron felt I could be trusted hence the reason he recommended me as the coach. I consider that an honor because the fathers of these boys were doctors, lawyers, Local businessmen and politicians. I was not paid and although I had to travel to Bridgetown twice a week, I loved every minute of it. My two sons Chris and Wesley were always with me on my coaching days. As the weeks went by, I had to make a decision about school for my children. I didn't want to take them back to Cambridge to get them into school because of the situation between my ex-wife and me. The law in New Jersey was, however, that if the children were of school age, they should be in school. I didn't care too much for the mother of my children anymore, but I loved my children dearly and I didn't want to lose them; it didn't matter then that I had taken the situation of us being together as a family for granted.

In the final analysis, I had to do what was best for them and I knew that they had to be in school. It was with great trepidation that I took my children back to Boston so they could attend school…a move that I have regretted to this day, largely because I now only have communication with my first son Chris. My other kids have no need for me and have not made any attempts to contact me; but I had created that situation, so I don't blame my children for anything.

When we got back to Boston my children were all in tears and I was also crying and there was great sadness between us all. It is an experience that I will never forget. When I got back to Salem, NJ, I was not the same person because I missed my kids a great deal and could not function properly without them there with me. Sometimes I would go back to Cambridge just to see them but when I got there, I would always have to go to the police station to have a law enforcement officer take me to the house.

I was only allowed to be there for a short time and it wasn't what I wanted; but ten minutes of hugging and kissing my children was better than no time with them at all. The worst part was when I had to leave them because it always broke my heart. This brought forth a renewed feeling of hatred towards their mother from me, and I didn't like the thoughts that came to my mind while I was there so I cut back on my visits. I learned from the police that there was now a restraining order against me from my ex-wife, so I could not go back to the house. To get around that, I had to park my car at my children's school and when they got out, I would go to them for a hug and a kiss. Eventually, I cut back on my trips to Cambridge. I broke off my relationship with Suzie, who I had stayed with when I brought my kids back from Boston to Salem, NJ. When I decided to breakup with her she didn't accept it as easily as I thought she would; she began to stalk me in a very dangerous way. She told me she would run me over with her car if she saw me with anyone else. I told myself that it was time to get out of Dodge. I was missing a lot of time on the job because of the uncertainty of my situation and eventually I was fired. The reason given was excessive absenteeism, however I was eligible for rehire and I decided to get away from Salem, NJ for a while and seek employment elsewhere.

To get away from Salem, I took a three-week job in Scranton, PA, and then I took another three-week job in Conshohocken before I went back to Salem. I was hoping Suzie would have calmed herself down by this time and she did. I got rehired at Salem for the third time. I was living in a world of uncertainty at that time and I became very depressed at different points in time. The main reason for my depressive moods was my not being able to be with my children.

Whenever I called to talk to my kids, my ex-wife would hang the phone up on me and that gave me a lot of stress, so finally I just quit calling. I received the divorce papers some time in 1977 and even though I was expecting it, I was crushed because deep down in my heart I felt there was a chance for reconciliation.

After receiving the papers, I had to accept the fact that reconciliation was far from her mind. What was strange in the papers was the fact that she didn't want any child support. All she wanted was the children. The State of Massachusetts had given her an uncontested divorce without any child support. I couldn't understand it, but I didn't question it. I decided to move on with my life. Women made my life bearable so I started dating heavily. First it was Bubbles, then there was Linda, and Beverly and then I ended with up Kathy. Kathy was not beautiful, but she was smart and I like having sex with her but she had a very sharp tongue and I had a very sharp tongue so it was a bad combination.

CHAPTER 23

CALIFORNIA, HERE I COME

Even though I had a job where I was making good money, had no problem with the ladies, had a nice apartment, I still felt like a looser and maybe I was. I decided I needed to find a way out; I wanted to find a new way because I felt that I was going around in circles in Salem, doing the same things over and over again.

My brother Dennis had moved to California from Michigan at the end of 1977. I always had the tendency to follow my mother, so at the end of the month, I sold everything I had and made plans with Kathy for her to follow me in a few weeks time.

I took off in my 1968 Pontiac Grand Prix and headed for California. When I went to Michigan I sold my Buick Wild Cat and bought the Grand Prix. It was a good running car and I felt that it could make the three thousand mile trip without any problems. Arrangements were made with my brother Dennis for a place to stay. There was a lot of work in California and, as a matter of fact, my brother Dennis was working at the San Onofre Nuclear Plant and there was an open call for welders at that location. The jobs were with the union and as a union member I expected to find work there as well. I left Salem heading south into Baltimore, Washington, then I got on the 81 Freeway straight into Knoxville, Tennessee where I took route 40 West into Arkansas. I drove straight into Oklahoma City where I spent the night. It was there that I started to think about the Western movies I had seen as a kid. The huge wagon trains, the cowboys fighting the Indians, and now here I was, traveling the same road that the Buffalo Soldiers traveled and where General Custer rode. All these thoughts took my mind off of my divorce and the possibility of loosing my children. It was good therapy for me. After a good night's rest, I took off early in the morning, staying on 40 west through the mountains, the valleys, and the plains. I had a CB in my car and my handle was the Peacemaker-Breaker One Nine. I was not afraid of the signs that said one thousand miles to here or there. I knew I was going to California, regardless of how many miles it would take to get there.

From Oklahoma City I hit Amarillo, Texas, then straight into Albuquerque, New Mexico. I did a little pit stopping in Flagstaff, Arizona where my worst fear was realized when I got a speeding ticket. I was doing great, driving and listening to the truckers and getting the information on where Smokey was laying out; but the troopers are smart; they caught me in a speed trap. I had to follow the trooper to the station to pay the fine. It was nightfall by the time I got through with the speeding ticket, so I decided to rest in Flagstaff.

I was almost there. It had taken me three days to get to Flagstaff but now I only had a few hours to get to California, and on to Los Angeles.

I was still on route 40 West and I picked up Interstate Fifteen South through the San Bernardino Mountains then into Pasadena then onto Freeway 10 West, which took me into Los Angeles, and into Harbor City where my brother Dennis had his home. I thank God I had made the trip safely in three and a half days; a trip that took the early settlers months and in some cases years to make. I was feeling good about myself. It was then that I came to the conclusion that a person with a college degree and a person with a skill could travel to any part of the world and find work.

I arrived at my brother's home safely and we had the usual greeting, a hug and a shake hand; the 'how was your trip' conversation. I was a bit tired but still sharp and as a matter of I was very excited about the whole situation. I was reintroduced to Adele and her daughter and I was shown to my room. The house sat on a corner and it was a ranch style four-bedroom house. I had the bedroom to the front of the house. I had left Salem, New Jersey on a Saturday and I had arrived in Los Angeles on a Tuesday. I had no intention of looking for work on that week. The job site was thirty five to forty minutes south of Los Angeles, but the union hall was another ten to fifteen south of the jobsite. The jobsite was on the Pacific Ocean of San Diego

The next day my brother took me to my mother's apartment. She was looking well and we hugged and kissed each other. She had broken up with her boy friend before coming to California and my mother was now a Buddhist at this time and she was and is an amazing person. She had the Gongyo down to a science. She said that she was not getting anything out of the Catholic faith so she made the switch to the Buddhist faith.

I stayed with my mom and talked for a while, then I went back to my room at my brother's house. He had told me nothing about a class action suit he and some of the other brothers who worked at the Nuclear Plant had against the company at that time and that a settlement was in the works. I thought that was his business anyway, although I didn't think I should have heard it from someone else. My main concern, however, was how this would affect my employment chances with the company, but I was not afraid because I knew I had a skill and my own transportation.

CHAPTER 24

MY FIRST JOB IN CALIFORNIA, SAN ONOFRE NUCLEAR PLANT

The following week, I visited the Union hall three times and I did not secure a job. Nothing was happening at the plant and they were sending out welders to other jobs. Most of the welders that went out were white so I was a bit concerned about whether I would get a job. On the days when I would go to the hall there were always two or three Black welders there trying to get sent out as well. The hall had a system where they had book one, book two, book three and book four. Travelers were on book four and quite often they never reached book three. The third week I was getting frustrated, but that was the week that I eventually got sent out and

I was very happy about it. I was truly happy because it meant that I could send for Kathy and we could have our own apartment; save some money and enjoy life in California. I still had to pass the welding test, though, which is what I did.

In the field, I was surprised to find quite a few Trinidad welders: David "2 sweet" Williams, Rocky, Shafiq Grafton, Padmore Mohammed, and Frank Sergeant ; to name a few. Bethel was the main contractor and the job had a few more months to be completed so it was touch and go, save all the dollars you can before this one job blows away.

I got an apartment not far from my brother's house; Kathy came to California and we started living together. I had a bank account but I never thought about investing money in any thing because I didn't trust the banking system ; I read too many stories about people getting ripped off by investment schemes so I was very skeptical. I had thoughts about buying a house but that did not materialize.

Thoughts of the curse were not giving any playing time, but thoughts of my children were constantly with me. When I called my ex-wife would still hang the phone up on me. I stopped calling, but I kept wondering if my letters were getting through. If she was cutting of the phone call, I figured she would do the same thing to my letters. Finally, I stopped the calls and the letters.

The lay-off did come after a few months, but I was happy about that because the driving to and from work was getting to be too tiring. I wanted to find work closer to home. Kathryn in the mean time had taken up accounting and she enrolled in a school in Los Angles.

She got financing and everything and I was happy for her. After the lay-off, I signed up for unemployment benefits. I also had a few thousand dollars saved so I kicked back on that. I had some time to do other things. I signed up for a course in bartending at a school on Hollywood Blvd. I even showed them the Mixology Certificate that I received from Harvard University and they couldn't believe it. It was a two-week course, and after graduation, I was sent to the world famous Century Plaza Restaurant. I was excited about that because this is where all the movie stars hang out and this was big to me...in fact this was huge.

CHAPTER 25

I DIDN'T GET THE JOB

I got to the restaurant about nine forty five that morning; the interview was scheduled for ten o'clock. Al, the restaurant manager, interviewed me. I cannot remember anything about him other than he was a short guy and he was white. The interview went well. I thought I had the job because he liked my background, the training I had from the Trinidad and Tobago Hotel and Catering School. My Harvard University two-week training course was also helpful plus my work history in the hospitality Industry. I believe all these led to his final decision to hire me. I was given a short orientation and I was going to be the back-up bartender. My bar was at the back and when the main bar got busy I was going to be the man the cocktail waitresses would come to for the over flowing orders. I wouldn't be able to see the stars but being in the same environment with them was thrilling and special to me. I started to reminisce about where I came from; about the times I embarrassed my parents my brothers and myself through my ugly actions. The stories I could tell my grandchildren if the Lord made that possible. I was tripping big time. My self-esteem was way up there. The stage was set; I was to report for work that evening at six: PM. I shook hands with the restaurant manager and took off to give the good news to those I was close to at the time. But my joy disappeared when I reported for work at six PM. I was there before six o'clock, but there was some confusion as to my employment. There was another bartender claiming that he was hired for the job and not me. The guy that said that he was hired to do this bartender job just happened to be white. I kept my cool. I went to the front to try to find the manager who gave me the job and who told me the position was mine; but he was no where to be found. I spoke to a white female who was in charge at the time, but she couldn't find my application to verify my claim to the position. When I went to the back, the other bartender was in position behind the bar. My first thought was; maybe they didn't want a Black man in that position. I wondered who was responsible for the fiasco. I could only say that it didn't sound right, it didn't look right and it was not right. Dejected and depressed, I left the Century Plaza Restaurant thinking that the curse was back.

The next day I went back to the school to find out who screwed up, but no one had a logical explanation for what happened. I was told that the position had been given to the other bartender the day before I took the interview. My response to that was YEAH RIGHT. I did, however, find work at the Tiki Club in Los Angles.

A Black man owned the club and on weekends the club was swinging. Although I was not making money, I still worked there for a few weeks and then I went back into the construction industry.

I found work through the pipe fitters union 250 of which my brother Dennis was a member. I was just enjoying life and taking one day at a time. My relationship with Kathy started to deteriorate and eventually we went our separate ways, because she would have killed me or I killed her if we had stayed together. Yes, it was that serious and as a matter of fact, she almost did try to kill me at one time.

I started smoking marijuana again after quitting in New Jersey. I was alone, because Kathryn had left me. I was heart broken again. I fall in love so easily and I always seem to get hurt but I always get over it only to do it all over again. Was I stupid or was I a glutton for punishment or was it a combination of both?

CHAPTER 26

CARIBBEAN DISCO PARADISE

My brother Dennis received his settlement money from the lawsuit and he used the money to rent or lease a building to open a nightclub. The club was named Caribbean Disco Paradise and he was the DJ. As a matter of fact, he was one of the best in LA at the time, bringing Calypso and Soca to the City of Los Angles. The business was going great. Our mom was the cook and she could cook her you know what off, but my brother in my view didn't have a good business head and he always wanted to blame others for his failures. I love my brother, but I didn't always agree with the way he handled things.

I was the bartender at the club and I had my brother's interest at heart. I was working for free, but my brother was set in his ways. I didn't know my brother very well before that time and I suppose the feeling was mutual

I gave up the bartending to pursue my dream of becoming a recording artist. I was still welding for the Union and I had about six grand saved up, plus I had vacation money coming from the union. I was in a good position financially and I even changed cars during that time. I bought a used 1972 Cadillac two door Coupe Deville, which was light blue with white interior. It was a nice car.

I started writing songs. I had written about ten songs but my first two were what I wanted to get recorded. I looked through the newspapers and found a piano player who wrote music and could arrange to have my songs copy written for a few dollars. I sent my first two songs *Disco Limbo* and *Come Back To Me* to get them set to music, but when they came back to me I choked. I was insecure about my singing voice, which I couldn't stand, so I had two options. One was to get voice training or to find someone to do the vocals. Either way, I was going to the studio to record these two songs. It was through my brother that I learned that Home Boy Alvin Cardinal was performing at the Roosevelt Hotel in Hollywood on Hollywood Blvd. In Trinidad, Vin Cardinal was a bandleader and a major entertainer. He had traveled all over the world entertaining and now he was in Los Angeles performing with Carlos Pueblos and his Quartet. Carlos was a master key board player for the band. I decided to go and see Alvin perform at the Roosevelt Hotel. I was in the place where some of my favorite actors had walked, eaten, drank and partied and their photographs were everywhere. John

Wayne, Humphrey Bogart, Rita Hayworth, Bob Hope, Frank Sinatra; I am sure you get the picture,: this was awesome to me. I had thought that the Century Plaza Restaurant was the closest thing I could come to as far as getting close to actors was concern but here I was in the lobby where these people stood at some point in their lives. This was big ; I was making history.

I got to the Show Room where Vin was performing. The room was packed but we still got seats close to the stage to see Alvin perform. Our small group, including my brother, met Vin when he was on break. Vin didn't know me but I was introduced to him as a songwriter from Trinidad. I was truly surprised when Vin acknowledged me during his performance and asked me to stand up so the people could see who I was. I got a great round of applause from the audience that was very outstanding to me, although it was just for a moment. I will never forget that and I felt great all evening. Alvin put on a great show, and before we left I made arrangement to meet with Carlos and Alvin to go over the two songs with the possibility of Alvin doing the vocal on both songs. I was thinking of doing background vocals along with two other female singers. The rehearsal went well and after that I made arrangements with a studio in Burbank to make my first ever recording. The cost of renting the studio was twenty-four dollars an hour.

Carlos was on key boards, a bass player and a guitar player who I had never met plus a drummer from Trinidad named Chili Charles who told me he was related to Mr. Charles, the ex head teacher from the San Fernando Boys RC School. Chili was good but I was blessed to have one of the world's best Tenor Pan players named Robert Greenwich on board. I had met Robert through my brother Dennis. The ensemble was in place and all the players were ready. We were going to go to the studio in three weeks but on the second week Alvin had to go to Israel to perform. I was a little disappointed but at the same time I understood his situation. Alvin was going to make more money performing in Israel than I could pay him to record my songs.

Studio time was seven PM. Everyone was on time and we were to put down rhythm tracks for both songs. I was going to do the vocal tracks with the hope that Alvin would be back in time to do the real thing. I was a complete novice as far as recording studios were concerned and I couldn't speak the music language. I didn't play an instrument, but I knew what I wanted to hear; I knew what I wanted my songs to sound like. Carlos was in charge and I trusted him because I knew he was good, but Chili was stubborn at times. We put down the tracks for Come Back to Me; a song I was inspired to write after my divorce. The tracks blew my mind. Robert's solo was fantastic even with a rough mix. On the second song came the problem with Chili he wanted one beat I wanted another. I wanted a Calypsoca beat ; he wanted a disco beat which was the beat at the time ; the Donna Summer, KC and the Sunshine Band kind of beat. I lost out in the end because time was being wasted just arguing about which way we should go so I gave in. I hated the beat after listening to the tracks that was laid down but I had to accept it because I just wanted it done. Besides, I had spent the money to do it and there was no turning back.

The engineers were already hired. I learned that these engineers were very clever in manipulating the situation in the recording studios and there is nothing one can do about it unless, of course, you have your own studio. The next six hour session which was to take place in two weeks was for lead and background vocals. It was decided that I was going to do the lead because Alvin was not available. The vocal work I was not impressed with but I was hoping to do better next time still in the end I was not impressed.. I had several copies of the rough mix done and I started shopping around for a label; without much success. I went to workshops with my demo and still got nowhere. I bought books on how to make and sell your own record, plus I learned a lot from the workshops. I finally ended up forming my own label KARIBBEAN FLAVA MUSIC   I was registered with BMI Broadcast Music Incorporated and I went back to the studio for another four hours for the final mix. I was not impressed with the final product. My one and only complaint was the lead vocals because I didn't believe my voice was right for the songs. I got the master tape, which I took to the pressing plant and one thousand records were produced and printed. I sold about one hundred, and I gave away another hundred. The record was a dud. I had spent over five thousand dollars and did not make any money from the attempt at stardom, but I had finished what I set out to do and that was my conciliation. My record was played on one radio station. It was played out of Santa Monica where a Trinidadian named Sandy Jules had a Saturday show lasting from noon to three PM. He was the only one to give me airtime. I thanked Sandy for that. I sent tapes and records to the other stations but not one of them played my music.

CHAPTER 27

LIFE GOES ON IN LA

I was working and things were going well for me at this point in time. I was a bit disappointed with my record sales but I had to live with that. I sold copies of my record at my brothers' club and it was there I met my name-sake, Mr. Mervyn Dymally, a highly educated black man from Trinidad and Tobago and brother to Bing Dymally whose alma mater was Presentation College. Bing is a friend of my brother Dennis and he was one heck of a soccer player. Mervyn was elected Lieutenant governor of California in 1974. I also had the pleasure of meeting Ms Esther Rolle, the actress from Good Times, Mr. Lawrence Hilton Jacobs of Welcome Back Cotter, Grady from the Sanford and Son show and Torian Blacque, the Hill Street Blues actor. They are all wonderful people.

My record didn't sell the million copies I was hoping it would, so I had to continue welding. The members and staff of Local 250 Pipe Fitters Union were very friendly so it was easy for me as a traveler, plus the fact that my brother was a member. I must mention one other member named Carl Hooven who is white. He treated me with great respect and I loved him for that. There were the twin African American brothers who were both pilots, a very unusual and special thing. We became friendly and some evenings after work and they took me flying with them over Los Angeles. The plane was a single engine and I believe we flew out of Compton.

My love life on the other hand needed some stability, but I almost didn't have to worry about my love life because I was bartending at my brother's club on Crenshaw Blvd one night. Kathryn was working as a waitress and although we were separated at the time; we were still dating of and on. There was this Super fly guy at the bar and Kathryn kept flirting with him. I was getting pissed so I took a break to go to the kitchen. Kathryn came in and we started arguing in front of my mother and others. We were face to face. I stepped on her foot and she pushed me away, then out of nowhere the knife came. She stabbed me twice once below my navel and once smack in the middle of my penis. The wounds were superficial and I didn't think she really wanted to fatally wound me. I believe that if she did, the wounds would have been much deeper.

I was truly lucky. I told myself I had to leave this woman alone; which is what I did. I hooked up with Hortense, a girl whom I met at my brothers club. After dancing with her a few times, I felt we had to be together. She was Bajan by birth and had lived in

England. She went to Nursing School in England and was now living in Los Angles with three beautiful kids. The kids were okay with me because I loved children. We started living together and it was okay for a while, but after six months, I had to terminate the relationship for reasons I don't remember. I just couldn't seem to make my relationships work and it was very depressing to me. I was already three years in California and it appeared as though I was not getting anywhere in life.

I had signed up at the El Camino College for an art class. I went two days then I dropped out. I took up learning the bass guitar. I started out great and bought myself a bass and an amplifier and started to play. I was getting good learning to read and play when all of a sudden I just dropped it.

It was not about money and I wasn't doing drugs. I just seemed to be losing interest in most of the things I found myself involved in at that time. I was getting tired of the United States and at the same time I was thinking heavily about Trinidad and Tobago. I was in a deep state of depression because of my divorce. Every thing else was just a front. I kept that front up pretty good, but I was hurting inside and found temporary satisfaction in song writing and relationships that did not work.

If it wasn't for my welding skill, I don't know where I would be today. I decided to change to another job and this time, I got a job in the San Fernando Valley at the Budweiser Brewery. It was at an expansion project for a company named C F Braun. There I met a Homeboy named Carlton 'Carly' Allen, who was a good welder and had worked in St Croix at the Hess Refinery before he came to America. We became good friends and it was at this project that I did some of my finest tig welding work. On the new job, I was given a fitter and a helper and we were given a twenty-four inch stainless steel Y that had to be welded to a flange bolted up to a huge stainless steel tank. The tank was about thirty feet high and there were three twenty-four inch welds to be made. The first weld was the flange and the weld was perfectly done. We then had to weld two twenty-four inch lines to the Y. The finished work was perfect also. The X rays were perfect and I was truly proud of myself after it was done. I started thinking back to when I was a young boy in Trinidad and my aunts were telling me how worthless I was.

I started crying. I don't know why. My fitter and helper, both white, wanted to know what was wrong with me. I told them it was something I just remembered, but I will never forget what my fitter said to me when we first met. He said and I quote:

"I am prepared to like you but you have the power to change that, I am also prepared to dislike you, but you also have the power to change that." Unquote!

After we were finished with the project...in my mind I was saying: how do you like me now? I did learn something from that experience, first, that I was a darn good welder and secondly, how easy Blacks and Caucasians can get along when it truly matters.

I met Robert Bailey sometime in 1982. He is the son of the great Trinidad and Tobago sprinter, Mac Donald Bailey. He had lived in England before coming to the United States and he was a professional musician and bandleader.

I decided to go to the recording studio with Robert, even though my first record was a dud. I had more songs to record, so we put down tracks for two more songs before Robert left for Trinidad. I had to put every thing on hold because I had Trinidad and Tobago on my mind also.

CHAPTER 28

THE RETURN TO MY ROOTS

My arrival at the Piarco International Airport was without ceremony. My father was there to meet me, which was good for me. I was detained at the airport because my passport had expired. My father knew somebody who knew somebody else so the wait was not long. After a while, I was allowed to leave.

The drive to Claxton Bay with my father was quiet. We did not seem to have too much to talk about after I had answered his initial questions. I didn't know where I was staying, but I was thinking that Mon Repos, the place I grew up was where I preferred to stay. I stayed at my father's house for a few days before I moved on to Mon Repos. I have traveled all over the United States as a welder and I always felt safe. But in Trinidad and Tobago, I felt a sense of freedom that I never felt in the

United States. Though I was apprehensive about my future, coming back home after being away for so long, I still had the feeling that I was going to be all right, perhaps because I was standing on the ground where my navel string was buried, and where my mother was born.

It was a feeling that I hadn't felt in many years and it was wonderful. Mon Repos was not the Mon Repos where I grew up with my cousin, Gail, and my other cousin, Patricia, who was a Down syndrome child and was still living at 27 Wooding Street. Patricia had aged but she was still sweet as ever and harmless as a lamb. Gail was planning to come to America because her mom was already there. She was married at the time to the son of Mr. George Weeks, the Trades Union leader and they had three beautiful children, two girls and a boy. Gail was a very good dressmaker. I was a little bit uncomfortable at the house but Gail was very nice to me the first week when I was just chilling and recovering from the jet lag.

Almost everyone I grew up with had left Trinidad. Others had just plain moved out of Mon Repos to live in other parts of the country, but my boyhood friend, Earnest Trim, was still there as well as Julian DYE Charles, one of the best soccer players that I ever played with. Winston Peggy Graham, a kid I hung around with had passed. My friend Conrad Peters was there. He had come back from Boston emotionally disturbed after his marriage had dissolved. My friend, Michael Clarke was still there, but that was it; all the other kids I grew up with were gone.

Mon Repos was a changed place and there was no life to it, not anymore. The Community Center was in shambles; the field where we played cricket and football and soccer was covered with weeds, three feet high. The Searchers Football Club had folded and there was no energy in the place. While at Mon Repos, I made a couple of trips to Port of Spain and that was where all the action was. I even went to Picton Road and Rose Hill Laventille after a visit to Port of Spain. I learnt that Tobago was the place I wanted to be because the government was refurbishing the Crown Reef Hotel and they would need help where running the hotel was concerned. I told myself: this was it.

My aunt Edna was still around, living in St Joseph Village, which is not far from Mon Repos. I went there and it was great to see my aunt (who is my mother's older sister;) again. We had a long talk about my life, my divorce and my children, my brothers and my mother. My aunt was a spiritual Baptist of the singing and shouting persuasion. She was in a church with a large membership; Leader Martin was the head of the flock. My aunt told me I needed cleansing and purging before I went to Tobago and I agreed. I didn't come back to Trinidad and Tobago with advanced credentials or a pocket full of money. If anything, I was more depressed and sad that my marriage had failed and I had the feeling that I never should have left Boston and my children behind. Even though many years had passed, I just couldn't get my children out of my mind. I felt that leaving Boston at the time was the right thing to do only because of the thought that I was entertaining which would have hurt them and me if I had given into them.

I was back in Trinidad and I had to focus on my life. It was a Friday morning when my aunt took me to the church to prepare me for the ritual. I had to fast for two days and two nights and I was placed in a back room with a dirt floor. There were bags spread on the floor; the only light came from the candles which were in the center of the room There were flags everywhere; black, green, white, blue, yellow. You name the color and it was there. I was given a bath that in Trinidad we call a 'bush bath'; it is taken with herbs and incense. It smelled awful but I felt it was going to do me some good. I dried myself off. I was given oils to rub over my body then I got into boxer shorts and I was given a robe to put on. My aunt covered my eyes with a white scarf, and then I was placed on the bags on the ground for fasting and meditation. I rested all day and night. I woke up the next day feeling hungry with my stomach growling, but I was feeling good and my aunt came to see me. She prayed with me. Then she brought me some juice and water. Leader Martin also came to visit me. I didn't realize that there were two other people who were next to me until leader Martin told me that three of us would be baptized the next day, which was Sunday. He also gave me two Psalms to read and he told me I must read them every day for as long as I live. They were Psalms 27 and 51. After reading I understood why he gave me these two Psalms. They were relevant and significant to my situation. They were appropriate to the turn my life had taken to the challenges and the obstacles, which I had faced and would encounter in the future. I had the feeling things were going to be better in my life.

The next morning I felt great. This was the day I was going to be baptized. I didn't come back to Trinidad and Tobago with any high expectations but I knew that somehow I was going to make it. I was an experienced welder and I was also a trained waiter and bartender and after that two-day-fast I was confident I was going to make it.

There was a little drizzle that Sunday morning but still the sun was ready to come out in its full West Indian splendor. My Uncle Joseph Shirley Atwell and his wife Doreen were present. All the church members were dressed in white. The high level sisters were dressed in a different color. Leaders from other churches were present and they all assembled at the church for prayer and thanksgiving. The actual baptism was going to take place at the Creek, which was about ten miles from the church, heading south. The Creek was part of the road that took you to Point Fortin, Siparia, and Cedros. After the morning service we took off in cars and vans for the big dip. The weather held up nicely and every thing went on smoothly. We got back to the church about twelve o'clock.

I don't remember eating though lunch was served and later on in the evening, there was the grand finale, with lots of singing and bell ringing. Preachers and preaching sisters were catching the power and falling all over the place. It was a very moving experience but I was quite apathetic about the whole event and was over anxious to see the conclusion. But there was this preacher who started to move me and I was in agreement with everything he was saying. I could hear myself saying: Yes, Yes, Yes and then suddenly, I felt the spirit moving within me and I started dancing. My aunt Edna came over to support me. I said: 'Don't touch me, don't touch me; I want Jesus to touch me; I want Jesus to touch me.'

That excited the whole church and even the preachers took their preaching to a higher level. The closing preacher was Leader Martin. He gave me my secret word and the hand sign that I should use when traveling. I was also given my colors. I had since forgotten the hand sign but I will never forget my password. I don't remember how it all ended. What I remember was feeling great. I felt as though a burden had been lifted. I felt as though an exorcism had taken place. I felt that I was ready to meet the challenges that came forth. I felt like a new person. I was ready for Tobago.

A few days passed and I said my good byes to my cousin Gail and the others I knew. I wanted to find my cousin Kenrick but no one knew where to find him. I will never forget him because but he was like a brother to me. Another kid I grew up with and wanted to see was Roger Clifton. He was a very nice young man and he was very protected by caring parents. With a little craziness, we would jump on our bikes and ride non stop to Princess Town and back, distance of some twenty miles east of Mon Repos. We wouldn't even be breathing too heavy after the long ride. When we hit the San Fernando roundabout we would be neck and neck like two sport heroes in a final race. It always ended in a dead heat. Roger was a nice young man and I trust that he is doing well today. Another friend that was missing was my best friend at Mon Repos RC School named Lloyd Jeff Lewis. Allan Nicholas, the George family, Ulric Sam Mitchell, Neville Walla Grant, who was my school mate and team mate in the Searchers Soccer Club were nowhere to be seen. As I planned my trip to Tobago, all these people came to my mind. I sat down under the coconut tree at the back of the house on twenty seven Wooding Street Mon Repos and reminisced about my childhood and my friends.

As I think back, thoughts of my cousin Ashley came to mind. He was only sixteen; he had a sharp mind and I am positive that if he had grown to be a normal person, he would become a math wiz. I saw that potential in him. He could sing and was very good at writing lyrics, but all that potential went to waste when he had a sudden mental break down which was attributed to Obeah, Voodoo.

The word was Ashley's grandparents on his father's side hurt him because they disapproved of the relationship between his father and my aunt. I never believed that it was Obeah that hurt my cousin Ashley and was told to shut my damn mouth because I didn't know what the hell I was talking about. The majority thought so the Obeah man was called in. He came with his sidekick and started digging a hole in front of the house. For what, I don't know. Around twelve midnight, they took Ashley to the cemetery to perform some kind of ceremony. Weeks after Ashley's condition got worse; he just lost it. Eventually he was taken to Port-of Spain and was registered as a certified mad person, crazy, that is.

The day before I left for Tobago, I went to Saint Ann's crazy institution to look for Ashley. He was registered there for almost twenty years. No one knew him and it appeared to me that no one cared. Some say Ashley is dead but if he is alive today he sure isn't trying to find anybody.

CHAPTER 29

RETURN TO TOBAGO

I arrived in Tobago on a Friday some time in July of 1982. I found a room within walking distance of the Crown Reef Hotel. The island had lost some of its tranquility. There were more cars on the road compared to the last time I was here in 1966.The beach close to the Hotel was crowded on Sunday. One of the strongest swimmers in Trinidad and Tobago was still. there. They called him Baker. He was the lifeguard at the beach at the time. He was also a good singer and guitar player, but I loved to watch him swim. We became friends. I also made friends with another brother named Anthony. Like Baker, he was six three, maybe six four; they both reminded me of my friend Durbin Crooks who was the chef at the BLUE HAVEN HOTEL when I worked there in 1966. Anthony had his own boat. We became friends on the very first day we met up and stayed friends until the last day I spent in Tobago.

Monday morning, bright and early. I was at the CROWN REEF HOTEL filling out application for the position of head waiter/ instructor. An interview was set up for another day in the week. Needless to say, I got the job. It was a joyous moment and time for me then to put the experience I obtained in the hotel industry to good use, thanks to Mr. Charles Solomon, the hotel manager, his assistant whose name I have forgotten, and my Immediate Boss Mr. Lator Thomas. These three men gave me the interview. Mr. Thomas I later developed a lot of respect for. The hotel was on the tail end of the refurbishing work so I had a few weeks to kill before opening day. I was so pleased with myself after the interview I set out for the BLUE HAVEN HOTEL at Bacolet Point. It was not the same. The beautiful landscaping was gone but the sound of the waves crashing up against the shore was still happening. The place looked deserted but I had met a brother who had leased the place and was in the process of refurbishing it.

But judging from the condition of the property, I knew it would take a lot of money to bring it back to prominence. The location was perfect for a resort and an ideal place for a vacation. After all, this was the place I worked fifteen years ago. This was the place I met Mr. John Mills, the British actor and his wife, and their daughter, Haley who was also an actor. Bringing the hotel back was a very good thing. Durbin was gone; so was Wiley the Bartender; Cool Cable the waiter had left the country; Johnston another waiter was doing something different and Bishop had gone back to Barbados. I learned all these facts from my friend, Leslie Saul, who was a waiter at the hotel in 1966. Saul was one of the coolest guys in the place at the time; he and Durbin Crooks gave me the most help and the most respect. They became my two best friends. Someone I met at the Crown Reef Hotel knew Saul. He was working at another hotel at the time.

When we met, it was hugs and smiles and hand shaking. Saul was still in good health and looking well we went out to have a few beers and to talk about old times. Leslie Saul was still a wonderful person.

Since I was out of the Hotel Industry for so long Mr. Solomon sent me to the Hotel Normandy in Trinidad for two weeks to sharpen my skills, to study the menus, the different dishes, and the different prices. The first day in the dining room I was shocked, at the manner in which the customer was treated. The waiters were rude and down right disrespectful to the guests. It was unbelievable! I asked myself many questions: why were these people hired to work here, why were they treating the guests in this way, how did they expect to make money by being rude to the customers?

It was obvious that management did not care about the customer's well being. Good service brings back customers; good food and lousy service just don't complement each other.   I decided to just observe, say nothing. At the same time, I was learning the how not to do it.   My stay at the Hotel Normandy led me to a nightclub on Frederick Street that held a gong show. I decided to enter using one of my own compositions, a Calypso entitled YOU HAVE TO WORK FOR IT. The rehearsal was great but I got gonged on the night of the show. I forgot my lyrics.

Back in Tobago, I started concentrating on the job, which was to train the dining room staff. There were nineteen women and two men. I was introduced as the headwaiter and instructor. I was loving it, but I decided there wasn't going to be any student teacher hanky panky. I could never be effective if I let that happen. I found a woman in a village near the hotel. I will name her C for now. She was just what the doctor ordered. She was about five feet five with pretty teeth, a beautiful smile and she had back; lots of it. C was my companion for the duration of my stay at the Crown Reef Hotel. The training was going great through the weeks and the months. I taught the basics: setting of tables, resetting, serving, and clearing. Everything I learned in my ten years in the hospitality industry, I passed on to the students. A wonderful bond had developed between us. I believed it stemmed from my past history at the Blue Haven hotel.

What really made my stay at the Crown Reef fulfilling was meeting Ms Muriel Donowa my teacher from the San Fernando Boys RC. She came to check my progress. I introduced myself to her. She told me that she was pleased with the work that I was doing and that made me feel real good inside. The hotel chef was a man named Joseph. His assistant was a young woman from Trinidad we called Big Bird. They were well trained in the culinary arts. The big day came for opening. All my people were ready and anxious to get into the swing of things. The party had a lot of government officials from Trinidad as well as Tobago. Included in the attendees a man I was angry with, Mr. ANR Robinson only because I felt that he was disloyal to Dr Eric Williams and the PNM political Party. What Mr. Robinson failed to understand was this; you cannot be a good leader if you are not a good follower. We shook hands for the first time and had a brief conversation. I was glad that we met. He appeared to be cool and charismatic but I still didn't like the way he dissed the Father of the Nation of Trinidad and Tobago. Loyalty is a rare commodity, and Mr. Robinson showed Dr. Williams no loyalty whatsoever. This is only my point of view.

I was enjoying the beautiful Tobago weather. The beaches were fantastic for sun bathing and swimming. I had left the sunbathing for the whites but I was doing a lot of swimming. I was truly enjoying my life at this point. I felt a rebirth mentally, spiritual, and psychically and I had developed a greater sense of morality and ethics both which were total strangers to me in the past.

The dining room staff was developing their skills nicely and I saw professionalism in a few. I was very impressed. Their attitude was totally different to what I experienced at the Hotel Normandy in Port-of-Spain. I didn't know any thing about Mr. Solomon, so I can't say much about him except that he made me laugh a lot because he was always cracking jokes. I liked him for that. The same was true for Mr. Thomas who was my immediate supervisor. He listened to my ideas and suggestions; he was a good man in my estimation. The dining room was in good shape but I was concerned about the kitchen. The food was not coming out fast enough for my liking. We had discussions about my concerns with the chef about how we could improve the situation in the kitchen, but things only got worse when the Chef got into a serious vehicle accident. The control of the kitchen was on the shoulders of Big Bird. She did a fine job but the young man who was her helper didn't know shit about cooking and I dreaded when Big Bird was off. I got very frustrated and I found myself getting into a lot of arguments with him. To make matters worst, I was ready for a change.

I was missing America and even though I loved the people of Tobago and I felt that they felt the same way about me, I was ready to leave. I had spent the greater part of eight months and did the best I could for the development of the hotel. There wasn't much more I could do. Besides I was missing my children back in the States even though I knew I had lost them. I wanted to see them any way. I had released all the devilish thoughts I was entertaining towards my ex-wife so I figured I could face her without having law enforcement intervention.

The manner in which I left my position at the Crown Reef Hotel was a little bizarre. It was over a half bottle of red wine left over from a party we had at the restaurant. I claimed the wine and a waitress made a claim for the same half bottle of wine. I drank it with my dinner and she got pissed off. The matter got to Mr. Solomon. I was called in to see him about the matter it was so insignificant that to this day I don't remember how it ended. What I remembered was crying my heart out on the day I was leaving. But what warmed my heart was all of the dining room and the kitchen staff were also in tears. It was a moment that I will never forget. I didn't realize that I was appreciated in this manner by the staff but NO MATTER HOW NICE YOU ARE EVERY ONE WILL NOT LIKE YOU. One Trinidadian employee I recall, never said any thing positive about me. I didn't know why staff members always came to me with what she said about me but it never bothered me because I had the love of the majority. I didn't leave Tobago after I left the Crown Reef. I hung out with my girl C.. We visited Bucco Reef, ate a lot, had plenty of sex, and swam a lot. I had a great time, but soon it was time to move on.   C and I departed promising to write each other every day. I wanted to marry her but she wasn't quite ready.   I worked a couple days at the Blue Haven Hotel for the brother who owned it at the time. I was highly compensated for my work.

CHAPTER 30

VIRGIN ISLANDS: HERE I COME AGAIN

I left Tobago in November 1982. I felt I was ready to meet the challenges that I was going to encounter in my life after the Crown Reef experience. I felt I was ready for anything but primarily because I was baptized and I felt that all my sins were washed away because of Leader Martin's prayers and counseling. Little did I know that I was venturing into the world of the unknown even though I felt prepared for what was ahead.

My plans where to spend a few months in St Croix, work the hotels and save enough money to go back to the main land; New York to be more specific. St Croix was not the same place I left in 1973. There were fewer people and not a whole lot of work. Hess Refinery was quiet. There were no plans for expansion and the tourist dollars were not flowing as freely as it was in the early sixties mid seventies.

I arrived on a Saturday and got a room in Christiansted, above a Spanish bar and restaurant. The rent was cheap and there were ladies of the night all around me. I didn't have a problem with that. Earl G. Robinson was still there. Fluent in Spanish and educated he was doing well, having risen from insurance salesman to ownership of his own firm. St Croix was just a stepping-stone for hundreds of Trinidadians who came to the island in the late sixties early seventies. Those who stayed saw growth potential in making there homes there. Kelvin Halls was still there as well another kid I grew up with in Mon Repos, San Fernando. The amazing Lune Alexander, my schoolmate, was still there and doing well. At the Hess Oil Refinery, hundreds left and hundreds stayed. It appeared to me that the animosity that was shown us by the indigenous people had vanished. The new Cruzans were the off spring of the so-called aliens that came there in the sixties and the seventies.

G Luz James was still the owner of the radio station WSTX but he was not spewing his venom on the masses of down island people as he did in the sixties on the radio. Now he sounded like a kinder, gentler person. I found work at a hotel in the east end of the island. The only problem was transport, which was solved when I learned that the hotel had a van that took employees back and forth to work. I was a waiter, a drop down from my position at Crown Reef Hotel where I was instructor/ headwaiter, but I am and adaptable person, so I just went with the flow.

I visited Grove Place, the Community where I left my family in 1973. A sadness came over me because I left them behind without much food and money. They trusted me to keep my word but at the time my word was no good. They suffered because of my actions, actions that I would pay dearly for. Three weeks after my arrival, I decided to go and find where the Trinis where living. I learned they had a pick up game every Sunday morning at a playing field in the village of Strawberry. Since soccer was my favorite sport and I was still in good physical shape, I found myself in Strawberry on a Sunday morning ready to play. It was my day off so I didn't have to worry about work on this day. I was happy to see old faces and acquaintances Sure enough, Earl G Robinson was present. Right away, I could tell that he was in a leadership position. We shook hands and greeted each other warmly. Earl was a good friend of my brother Tony. I had great respect for the young man because I remembered him in Mon Repos walking to school every day from St Joseph village where he lived. Presentation College, San Fernando was a long walk, maybe seven or eight miles one way. Seeing where he came from to where he was at that point and time in his life, I would consider that a triumph for him. There is only one person I often wish I was like and that person is Prince Charles. As for Earl, I have pure admiration and respect for the brother; always will.

I was ten weeks into my stay on the island and was pretty much ready to go back to the mainland I was always in touch with my brother, Tony, who was living in Brooklyn at the time. He was also keeping my union dues up to date. Through him I learned that there was an open call for welders at the Limerick Pennsylvania Nuclear plant. The union hall was in Philadelphia. He was making plans to go to that job. I hade decided to I was going to wait until Spring to make my move.

The hotel started downsizing, so that was it for me. I was a little disappointed but that was the nature of things. I soon found work at the King Christian Hotel Restaurant. It was early March 1983, but my money was funny. I couldn't make the move just yet because I didn't have enough for my plane ticket.

Then it hit me: it was a Sunday evening. A pain just below my heart came from nowhere and grabbed me. It was very scary. It was my day off, too. I had played almost ninety minutes of soccer that morning, had a couple shots of Babash drink and drank a couple of beers, and was feeling great. I wasn't taking any kind of drugs. Where the hell did this pain come from, was my thinking? I played pool and dominoes at the corner bar for hours before I went to my room that evening. Then I started thinking: this couldn't be natural. I still had remnants of my original thinking floating in my mind, in spite of my baptism. I had thought that the change was instant and permanent.

St Croix was the place where I did a lot of good, but all of my deeds were not noble ones. I was not a responsible person and didn't realize it. I was selfish and self-centered. You know the saying "what goes around comes around" There is no way around that. I hurt a lot of people there mainly my wife and children. Now it was time to pay the price for my selfish actions. I could've gone straight to Brooklyn when I left Tobago but my punishment was waiting for me in St Croix.

The ambulance took me to the Sunny Isles Hospital. I was still in a lot of pain. I was taken to the Emergency Room. I sat there; one hour, two hours; no relief was in sight. After five hours, there was still no attention. Perhaps it was because I had no insurance. I don't know. Usually that is the case. Five hours into my stay and still no relief. I was moaning and groaning. The pain was that severe. I would fake a sick to stay home from work, but this was totally different. I was hurting and didn't know what was hurting me. All I could say was 'Oh God! Oh God!' But I believe he was out blessing some people some where for the good that they had done and was waiting for me to complete my punishment phase and there was no way around it.

After six hours of pain, I finally had a brief moment with a doctor and I mean that literally. He recommended some sort of painkiller and then was gone. There was no examination; nothing. To this day, I don't know what he gave me, but just like that, the pain was gone. Was it the medication or did the demons decide to take a smoke break? I don't know. I left the hospital very concerned about my health and about my future. I had no savings, no stocks or bonds, no asset; nothing really. If I should die then, what would become of me, I asked myself? A pauper's burial would be my only option and still some might say I didn't even deserve that.

I love St Croix. This is the island where I saw the sunrise and the sun set on the same day. A white couple I became friendly with took me to the Sunset Flash on one of my days off. They took me to a spot on the eastern road. We drove towards the water until we couldn't go any more. If we did, we had a fifty-foot drop to contend with. The rocks at the bottom of the cliff didn't look very inviting. We parked, got out and waited. It was the most glorious sunrise I had ever seen in my life. It made my hair rise. The big beautiful orange colored sun in all its splendor, seemed to be looking at us as we looked at it. You can look directly at the sun right after it lifts itself from out of the water. That's the impression you get when you get the first peek. It looks as though its in the water. Anyway, I got hooked. I instantly became a sun man, even a sun worshiper.   When I saw the beauty, the power, the magnificence of this orange ball of fire lifting itself towards the heavens, I said Thank you Jesus! Thank you Jesus!

On the very same day we went to Fredericksted, which is the west end of the island to view the sunset and it was seeing that illusive flash that I truly became an official Sun Man. It was illusive because I was told it took days, in some cases weeks to see the flash. Conditions must be perfect. Some times clouds get in the way, making it impossible to see it. But every one should take the time whenever possible to see the rising and the setting of the sun. There is a bar on the beachfront north east of the Fredericksted water front. Frequented mainly by whites, there were a few times when I passed by usually in the afternoon around sunset time. They were applauding now. I know why they were applauding. It was the flash they were applauding. The flash truly is a moving experience; it was for me.

I still had my job at the restaurant and was doing a few extra hours for Hershel who owned a restaurant on a tiny island that was also home to the fifty room Hotel Bagga. A Trinidadian Pan maker was the leader of a five-piece ensemble that played for Hershel on weekends. I worked on those nights. Another Trini brother named Masai was lead tenor Pan player in the group. I made heavy tips on those nights but I was ready to go. In fact, I was getting restless; still I was short on the funds for my plane ticket.

I had called my brother Tony and my cousin Gerald Bacchus, a kind and wonderful human being, who told me he could house me for a couple weeks when I got to the States until I found work. It was mid February and I was enjoying myself, swimming and snorkeling on the cay. But I was not making enough money to make it work for me. I was missing my children very much and wanted to see them real bad; besides, I wanted to put my welding skills back into play.

With the help of Earl G. Robinson, I had my ticket to travel back to the States. It was almost the end of March when I said goodbye once again to the beautiful Island of St Croix. I was going to come back but I just didn't know when at that point in my life. I had come full circle and was going around again for the second time. This time, though, I was going to make it. That was the way I felt. I had my colors, I had my password to chant on, I had my little pouch with stuff Leader Martin gave me to pin to my jockey shorts. I didn't know what was in it, but Leader Martin gave it to me so it had to be good. Once again, I was venturing into the unknown, but I felt that I was ready for the second go round so I said ::Mervyn let's go do this thing.

CHAPTER 31

AMERICA, I HAVE COME TO SEE YOU AGAIN

The band was in ripping form. The back up singers were in beautiful harmony and I was belting out a Calypso. The audience and myself were one. The applause was deafening. When I woke up every body on the plane was applauding but the applause was not for me: it was for the pilot and the crew of the aircraft.

I was asleep and dreaming when the plane landed safely at the Kennedy AirPort in New York. My cousin Gerald and my brother Tony were at the airport to meet me. We drove directly to my cousin Jerry's. It was a Saturday the temperature was around 45 degrees and sunny. I was greeted warmly by my cousin-in-law, Nova, Jerry's wife, and their first two beautiful children, Sheldon and Greer. Both are college graduates today. Sheldon is an airport traffic controller and Greer is a math teacher. All are doing well. It has been almost a year since I did any kind of welding and I was very anxious and concerned about my performance on the welding test because I knew I had to be one hundred percent on my welding test because the Limerick PA job was a Nuclear Plant. All work must be of nuclear quality. As good as I thought I was, I still needed to practice at least one week in Tig and Stick welding. I was praying and chanting for a break but the break that I had coming was going to be highly spiritual and enormous I could even say HUGE.

My brother Tony was in my corner; so was my cousin, Jerry and his family. I could not fail. It took me two weeks to hook up with the union hall to get clearance for a referral for the job. I was lucky there was still an open call for welders and fitters. Tony was already working at the site and was staying in Pottstown, PA, a small community not far from Limerick. There were quite a few brothers from Local 638 as well: Elias Alexander Disco Pete the DJ, Fitzroy Gill, just to name a few. On the second week after my arrival, my brother Tony came to get me to take me back to Pottstown with him. His son, my nephew, Earl Greaves, was staying with him at the time. Today Earl is a towering six footer with dreadlocks writing poetry and lyrics for songs but at this point, he is just a scrawny little young man enjoying his life with his father and his mom Jackie.

I had to go to the union hall in Philadelphia. Monday morning we arrived in Pottstown from Queens, New York about nine PM. I had shaken off all the jetlag from St Croix to San Juan, to Miami, to Kennedy Airport. I was still worried about the welding test. I wanted this job badly. I wanted to hit the ground running.

Monday morning; I was up about four AM to hit the road for Philly. It was close to a two-hour drive. I wanted to hit the hall early as well as beat the traffic on the highways.   I arrived safely at the hall about seven o'clock. The hall was packed. There was a lot of work going on in the Philly and surrounding areas. There were still vacancies to be filled at the Limerick jobsite. I breathed a sigh of relief when I learned that. When it was my turn to sign up, my name was on the list. Welders were in demand, so that was a good thing. I had my referral in hand by nine o'cleck, and was ready to make the trip back west to the Limerick job site. I was excited, very excited. I didn't go to the job until the next day. I had called the job site to inform them of this, they were cool with that.   I rested at my brother's apartment in Pottstown, prayed and chanted a little and counted my blessings, looking towards the future basically embracing silence.

Tuesday morning, bright and early, I was at the job site with referral in hand I met and chatted with a few brothers, asked about the test, had some small talk, welders conversation: was the test a hard one, was the inspector mean, was he lenient, was it a bend test or X-rayed? Things that you feel that would give you and edge when you get into the test booth.

I arrived at test shop about five of seven, met the shop steward and gave him my referral and union card to verify membership and union dues status which included your social security number. It was 1983 and no drug test was necessary as it is today. With all my documents in order I was sent to the welding inspector's office. When I got there I had a delightful surprise waiting for me. The man who was in charge of the test was none other than Randy Poole, the shy young welder I met in 1973 at the Salem Nuclear Plant in Salem New Jersey. Great day in the morning! After mutual recognition, we hugged each other, shook hands and hugged again. Everyone in the place stared, out of curiosity, I suppose. The place was crowded. We both regained our composure and proceeded with the business at hand; the welding test. Lord knows I was feeling great already, almost to the point where I felt I had the job already. I had changed that way about me, taking people and things for granted. I had cleansed myself of that mentality and accepted the situation of actually passing the test in order to be hired. You were paid for testing in those days. You came to the shop for four to six hours of testing. If you don't make it, you still got paid for the time you were there, that is not happening today.

Randy didn't owe me anything. All I did for him at the Salem job was give him a few pointers pertaining to welding because I saw he had the potential. Nevertheless, he was telling everybody that I taught him to weld but I knew he was just being kind and modest. He had come to the Salem Plant as a welder, but still he giving me credit for helping him. That gave me a strong feeling of pride and value. Randy Poole, in my view, was a kind and wonderful person, a person that I will do almost anything for. I don't have to mention it, but I passed the welding test with flying colors. The unusual thing about the whole scenario is the fact that I spent two weeks in the test shop after completing three coupons, in three days, all perfect on the x-rays. Welders were coming and going left to right, but I was still in the test shop. It was a fantastic experience for both of us MEANING Randy and myself. But like they say, eventually all good things must come to an end. I had to go to the field to weld pipe for the Bethel Construction Company. Almost every lunch period I was in the test shop chatting with Randy. We would talk about old times and experiences that will stay with me for as long as I live.

The thing about our friendship was that we never socialized. We met a few times for a couple of beers but that was it. I knew our friendship was job related, but as I said before, it is one that I will cherish for as long as I live. There is something that always bothered me; the open harassment that seemed to have been targeted at minorities.

Latrines on most construction jobs had things written about Black people- nigger this, nigger that. Everywhere, every latrine every job had the insults written in plain sight and often in graffiti. I fought it by constantly by telling myself they were not talking about me. It told me that bigotry and racism were everywhere and I didn't have the power to make them go away so I had to brainwash myself into believing that they were not talking about me. I will never forget the ONE that said. YOU KNOW HOW TO STOP FIVE NIGGERS FROM RAPING A WHITE WOMAN IN DETROIT….. JUST THROW THEM A BASKETBALL. When you write something like that about a race of people, you not only stereotype the whole race; it shows that you have some deep seated hatred that you need to let off

Things were going very well for me. I was planning to buy a car. I couldn't buy a new one because I had damaged my credit so I was saving up for it. I was going to pay cash and I needed twelve hundred dollars the car dealer wanted that much for 1973 Olds Delta 88. Three weeks into the job, I bought the car for nine hundred dollars. I had obtained a Pennsylvania driver's license. I was ready to hit the road. I tuned the car up put new tires on changed the oil; the works. My first road trip was to go to Boston to visit my children. In the middle of May, I went to Boston. It had been six years since I had last seen my children. I got their number from my brother Tony. He never lost contact with them. I arrived in Cambridge, Massachusetts around one PM. My ex-wife had changed apartments. They were now living in the apartment at the front of the complex, which is on Western Avenue, not far from the world famous Western Front nightclub. I went up to the second floor apartment not knowing what to expect. When I knocked on the door, my ex-wife opened it. She had gained quite a lot of weight but what really damaged my heart was when I saw my last two children with her. Abu and Kurleen were hiding behind her. I knelt before her to make eye contact with my daughter and my son. They will not come to me. They acted as though I was a total stranger to them. I knew they were brainwashed. I knew I had lost at least two of my children. My first two sons, Chris and Wesley, were not at home at the time. I stood up and asked her what had she done to their minds, and then I left, got in my car and headed straight back to Pottstown, PA, hurt and sad. But I took full blame for it: I was responsible for what had just happened.

I started dating a sweet young thing named Amy. She was Black and a nurse's aide at a local hospital. She had two children that were beginning to like me but I had to terminate the relationship after three months because she smoked and kept a dirty house. How one can be a nurse's aide and be so filthy is beyond my comprehension.

I was making several trips a month to New York to visit friends and relatives. My friend, Trevor LaRode, was always my main stop. Trevor was working in the City. He was also a member of Local Union 638. I was still trying to avoid working in the city, but my brother Tony was always telling me that I would have to do it to build my pension as well as vacation money. In other words, he was saying it was in my best interest to work in New York. I told him after my current job, I would give New York a shot. My brother and I were doing good work, So much so that they had us in the jobsite monthly Newsletter. The headline was TWO BROTHERS FROM TRINIDAD and TOBAGO. There was photograph of me and my brother on the front-page standing side by side. I had my right hand draped over my brother's left shoulder. The story was brief.; when we got into welding, our children, hobbies etc. That was wonderful. It was sensational, to say the least. It was a moral booster for both of us. We took every thing in stride.

We moved from Pottstown to Amityville. My brother was reluctant, but he did it any way. Amityville was about five miles east of Pottstown. We got new furniture. We had a two-bedroom apartment. Life was good. I had sufficient working hours to qualify for medical and dental coverage so I did some dental work, putting a gold star on one of my upper front teeth. Then I had lower partials put in. It accentuated my smile. It made me look good. But there was a lot of stainless steel in the work had an adverse effect on my health. A month after I had the work done, a rash consumed my whole body from my neck down to my feet. It was so ugly I would've killed myself if I had a gun. That's how serious it was. I went to see a Pottstown doctor. He didn't tell me what it was but my first thoughts were: curse the demons from hell; they had caught up to me again. The doctor gave me a black soap to bathe with three times a week. He also gave me some pills. Where did this evil demon with the diabolical intentions come from? How did it find me? These were the questions on my mind, to which I could find no answers.

After eights months on the job, the threat of layoff was in the air. This is when you start to tighten your belt and stay within your budget. My brother Tony went first. I thought it strange since he was hired before me. Tony did not hesitate. He went straight to the Oswego, New York Nuclear Plant. There was an open call for welders and pipe fitters. I was going to make the same move as soon as I got my pink slip. I'd rather be working instead of collecting unemployment benefits!

My lay off came two weeks after my brother's. I called the local union that was manning the job about employment. The word was: come on up we can use you. I felt great at this point. I didn't need a whole lot of downtime because we had bills to pay. I was also thinking about going back to the recording studio to lay down tracks for- *Bulb In The Sucket* -and *CooYah Mouth*-two of my compositions I had high hopes for.

Things don't always go as planned. I got laid off on a Thursday. I called Tony to let him know about the situation. He and a couple other brothers had rented a two-bedroom apartment in an all white community. He would put me up until I got the job. I had the option to share his room or find my own accommodation when the time came. This was per our phone conversation. The Sunday evening I arrived in Oswego to the given address from my brother; every thing was cool. When I got there we shook hands talk a little had a couple beers then I fell into a nap. The trip was long and I was tired from the driving. Unfortunately I woke up to hear my brother Tony on the phone in conversation with our younger brother Dennis who was living in California at the time. Tony was telling Dennis that I was such a burden on his shoulder.

More was said, but I think it is unnecessary to print since my brother has passed. I got up went to the kitchen where he was having the conversation. He was a bit surprised at seeing me. I asked him if that was the way he felt about me. I was hurt and angry at the same time. I didn't hesitate. I picked up my bag and headed back to Amityville. In one week's time, I sold the furniture and headed to Brooklyn. Tony had taken everything that he owned from the apartment and it gave me the impression that he was not going to return no time soon. I did leave some unpaid bills behind but what I did hurt my brother's Tony's credit. His credit was impeccable and I always wish I was like him in that respect. He corrected it eventually but he was pissed at me for what

I had done and didn't speak to me for months after the Oswego incident. I was pissed at the way I thought he felt about me which moved me to do what I did. I was his older brother, for crying out loud. We are family. I came to work and make money. Why are you dissing me like that, was my feeling.

CHAPTER 32

UNION 638 UNITED ASSOCIATION NEW YORK CITY, NEW YORK PIPEFITTING INDUSTRY

After much resistance, I decided to work out of my home Local. I had called my two friends who were brothers; Trevor and Vernon La Rode, to inform them that I had made the decision to come to work in New York. They were living there at the time. They were always encouraging me, as did my brother, to come work in NYC for the obvious reason; my pension, 401k, medical and dental benefits. I always resisted telling them there had to be a better way. At this time, I was thinking of radio and broadcasting. While I was working at the Limerick Plant I took a few classes on Saturdays for Disc Jockeys and was getting good at it.

The school was based in Philadelphia and it was more like an outing for me. I looked forward to Saturdays. I was enjoying it.

I drove into Brooklyn on a Monday. It was easier to find housing during the workweek. I went straight to an agency some where on Flatbush Avenue. I found a room in a private home. It was ninety dollars a week. I had over a grand in my pocket, so money was no problem. The home was on New York Avenue, not far from Faragut Road. The agency had called and informed the homeowner that I was coming. There was no doubt in my mind that my union membership helped in me getting the room. My appearance also helped. I was neatly dressed as I always tried to present myself in a respectable manner. To make a long story short, I got the room. It was on the third floor. It actually was an attic converted into two rooms. There was another tenant living in one room but I was lucky; I had the room facing New York Avenue.

It was perfect for me. I settled in nicely. I was going to make it here. The rest of the week found me visiting friends and family, getting information about the jobs that were available. The thing I learned about my home local many years ago was, there wasn't a hiring hall. It was my firm belief that it was so because this was a way to screen potential hands. Almost every other local in the association had a hiring hall that includes Canada. Why not my local?

The following week, I set out to *'shape'* the different jobs in the city. *Shape* is the term used for actually going to the job sites to show your union card and to let them know that you are available for work; you also leave your name and telephone number. If they need you, they call you but most times, they never call.

My first job in the city was with a company named Alfa. My friend Vernon was instrumental in helping me obtain that position. It was a three-month project requiring lots of welding. I liked that but there were other aspects of the job that I was not happy with. I remember making a weld on the fifth floor of a high-rise building. The foreman came and stopped me from welding to let me know that a delivery truck had come with supplies for the company and I was needed downstairs to help with the off loading. I was pissed, but then it hit me that this was my first job. Besides, my friend Vernon spoke for me and I didn't want the company to view him as someone with bad judgment. So I sucked it in and went down to help unload the vehicle. It was then that I learned that all jobs in the city were the same way. I had to make a quick adjustment to my work ethics. Every other job I worked at was different. There was an expeditor commonly called a runner. He and one apprentice and perhaps a pipe fitter took care of all the materials when they come in so all the off loading I was doing was new to me, though it was an adjustment I was prepared to make if I was going to make it in the city.

I was beginning to like it in the city after three months. I was getting into the mainstream of things and I was asking myself why didn't I do this before. I knew the answer to that question. I was praying and chanting a lot because I didn't know what to expect. Also, I wanted to change my ways, change my life, change the way I did things. I didn't want to be a deceitful hypocrite; I wanted to be a man of integrity, a man that can be trusted; a man of substance. I did less than three months on the first job, the second job lasted another three months with another company. All this time, I was developing a side of me that I didn't know. I had picked up a cause that became part of me. I didn't care about any drugs, never did, even though it was all around me but the South African situation got hold of me in a way that I could not explain. I had Mandela Posters, Free South Africa, and End Apartheid signs all over my room. I started to wear buttons relevant to the situation. I went to Free South Africa Rallies in Manhattan. I was beginning to question the morality of the United States, Britain, and her allies who have billions of dollars invested in a country where you have four million whites governing fifty millions Blacks. What kind of Democracy was that? I knew they would say it was in their country's best interest. More significantly for me, the oppressed people were Black, so it was easy for them to do what they were doing. Some whites say Blacks were irrelevant so that makes it right.

I went through one job after another without any problems. I had three different girl friends between January and October of 1984. Two went back to Trinidad. One was married but didn't tell me about it until her husband came to the States. She was just saving up for his plane ticket. It shocked me because I was falling in love with her. It made me suspicious of all women. Then I did the wrong thing. I labeled all women as gold diggers, and users of men. But what would you call a man who was a womanizer? I seriously wanted to change that way about me and I was seriously thinking about marriage at this point in my life.

I had worked almost ten months out of my home Local. I learned quite a lot from my white Union brothers, but I hated the work ethics of my Black brothers who were also union members. They were straight up back stabbers who always wanted to outdo the white members. Some of the Blacks worked so fast that they actually turned a ten-week job into a six-week project. Most of the whites didn't like that, but those guys didn't care. One white worker told me when they let us [Blacks] in the union every thing changed. I was in total agreement with that, after studying the work ethics of my Black brothers. They were good welders and pipe fitters, but it seemed as though they always have to prove to Massa how good they were. The old slave mentality was still alive and well. I was just disgusted with those who just thought they were above all suggestions, especially coming from another Black.

I worked at the white worker pace. I developed an easy going, don't rush me attitude. If the white welder made six welds, I was going to make six welds. The only difference was my welds were going to look better than his; that was it. I didn't make a lot of friends amongst my Black union brothers because I was very vocal in my resentment towards their work ethics.

1984 came and went. I had lots of money saved up and was looking forward to going back to the recording studio to put tracks down for two of my compositions. I hired the late Tony Codogan, a brother from Barbados who was educated in music. He was my arranger who later became my friend. Tony was going to teach me to play the piano. He was a good man. In the mean time, my brother Tony had bought a home in Syracuse, New York. He was still working at the Oswego Plant. My mother, who was still living in California, decided to move to Syracuse to live with my brother who had a nice home on Lincoln Avenue. She eventually moved to Kennedy Square Apartments on Water Street.

I was totally into the main stream of things. I learned the train system, the bus route; I learned Harlem and the Bronx, the theaters, and movie houses. Sunday was my favorite day to go to Forty Second Street and Times Square early morning to have breakfast, take in a show, check out the X-rated movies, do a little shopping, have lunch, and take in another movie. I loved Sundays in Manhattan and I was beginning to love New York. It was some time in February 1985 that my friend Vernon introduced me to a Trinidadian beauty. I will call her Ulah. He took me to meet her. She had an apartment on Farragut Road and New York Avenue. The first time I saw this beauty I knew this was the woman for me. We exchanged greetings. She was warm and cordial and smelled nice. Her apartment was clean. The ambiance in the apartment gave me the impression that she was a woman with good taste with a touch a luxury. When Ulah went to the refrigerator to get us a couple of beers, there was no doubt in my mind when she bent over to reach the beers that this was a woman that I wanted to stand behind literally. I was ready to get married. Before Vern and myself left Ulah's apartment, I had her number and mailing address. We made a date for the following Sunday. Time Square was not going to see me that Sunday; Ulah was.

The meal was great. We had crabs and callaloo, white rice, stewed brown, chicken salad, boiled plantains, and sweet potatoes. The beverage was Sorrell ; desert was cassava pone with Vanilla ice cream. After that delicious meal, I was full. In one of the Mighty Sparrow's Calypso Ivy told John 'you can't make love on hungry belly'. Well, let me tell you; you really can't make love on a full belly. Even though I knew she was ready for love, I was not.

First impressions were very important, I always knew that and practiced it well. We chatted for a while, but she didn't tell me every thing that I felt was important. It wasn't any thing that was going to change my mind about her, but I felt she should've told me from the GET GO. I had to learn from another source that she had three children two boys and one girl. Danny was the first-born. He was a United States Marine. Jemma, was the daughter. I was warned to watch out for her, SHE MOUTH HOT, using island lingo, and she cuss out she-mother on Nostrand Avenue. The last child was Kelly. He was living with the mother but had gone to DC to visit his aunt. That explained the other room in the apartment, which looked like a teenager's room. Why was this person telling me all this? My mind was already made up ; this was the woman for me. People just like to gossip and I hated gossip.

Two weeks after we met, I gave up my room on New York Avenue and moved in with Ulah. I usually give a new relationship three months. If the feeling is still fresh after three months, I believe the relationship stands a good chance to work. With my new frame of mind regarding life and friendship, I believed that this relationship was going to work. I felt that the Lord had answered my prayer. I was praying for someone to love and someone to love me, but not always sure of my feelings towards females, it took time for me to really know how the other person felt about me. Ulah and I were getting to like each other. I was going to be loyal to her. She was single, but she had just gotten divorced. It was going to take time for healing on her part. She needed time to shake off the hurt and disappointment of a divorce. I was willing to give her that time.

Ulah was running a SU- SU one hundred dollars a week. I took two hands. I needed extra money for the recording studio. There were twelve hands in the SU-SU. I was way down the line for a hand but that didn't worry me. I was working. I had vacation money. I was in good financial standing, for the first time in my life, so money was no problem. I was going to do everything possible to make the relationship work.

Kelly and myself were getting along well. He was a quiet, good-looking young man. He looked as though his father was Portuguese but he had the lying and stealing curse just as I had as a young man. I knew that if I could stop stealing and lying any one could. Kelly was just fifteen going on sixteen. He had time to change his ways. I was prepared to help him in any way that I could.

We were into the third month of the relationship and still going strong. Ulah was not only a good cook; she was also a hard working woman. She worked nights at a nursing home in Manhattan. She never missed any time from work. She was, in my view, a reliable employee. During the first three months of our relationship, I met her daughter and her first-born, Danny. The daughter had a one-year old girl child, cute as a button. Danny was planning to get married. He was stationed in North Carolina. He was a very respectful young man and reminded me a lot of my first born who was also a United States Marine; quiet, strong, and confident. Danny and I hit it off well. I was meeting some of Ulah's friends. Some I liked, a few I could do without only because of the gossiping, which was all they did.

I made a very serious religious change when I met Ulah. She was a chanting Buddhist. I didn't join the church because of Ulah; I joined because my mother was a member. I was truly impressed with my mother and how fast she picked it up. She knew the whole book by heart and she took what she was doing very seriously. On the other hand, I was finding it difficult to learn. I was getting up early a couple of mornings a week to go to the church in Manhattan for service. Ulah had a white girl friend who was a member and we went to her house one day a week for service. I completely gave up everything Leader Martin taught me but I didn't abandon anything. I was into the chanting. Maybe I was trying to impress Ulah, but the events that took place in my life from that point when I made that religious change were both fulfilling and disastrous at the same time with a near death experience. This was when I believed that the demons with diabolical intentions had caught up to me again and had every intention of destroying me. It was then I started to think I made a very serious mistake when I deviated from every thing

I embraced. The leader gave me certainty when I asked Jesus to touch me that Sunday night with that emotional out burst; I felt that he did. That night, I felt a feeling that I know I will never feel again, and I just gave it all away to something that I had no understanding of.

Ulah had her own car and sometimes we took trips to Washington, DC, using her car. We were beginning to trust each other. We were both becoming predictable. We were beginning to enjoy each other's company so much so that I was thinking marriage, but there were still obstacles in the way, dogging the possibility for any legal union between us.

I was patient like I said before. She had just gotten out of a marriage through a divorce and I felt that it was only fair to give her time to get over that experience so I decided to give that question a rest.

CHAPTER 33

THE MOVE FROM FARRAGUT ROAD APARTMENTS TO BROWNSVILLE, NEW YORK, A NEW HOUSE, A NEW BEGINNING

Ulah was very proud of herself. She was beaming with pride and I was very happy to be part of it. She was a very hard worker and I respected her for that. We both worked to make the house a home. When it was done, Ulah's home was elaborately furnished. She was a woman of good taste, perhaps a little too expensive for my taste.

In the mean time, I was going from job to job, nothing unusual, I must say. It was the nature of things, so I had no objection to it. I worked at the Trump Tower, Columbia University, Wall Street, Park Avenue, and the Twin Towers, to mention a few. It was a very exciting time for me. I became a student at a radio broadcasting school in Times Square. ATS Announcers Training School was the school where a very popular Trinidadian DJ got his training.

I had decided to get out of the construction industry and get into a softer more challenging way of making a living. Classes were three nights a week. From work I would head straight to school. I was dressing nicely for work and for school. If you ride the subway, you want to look clean and tidy because you never know who you may run into, but when you go to work looking clean, I find some of your co-workers may and or will ask me if you're going church or going to work. At least, that's what happened to me. Sometimes, my co-workers would ask me if I was a pimp or some other stupid questions that really annoyed me. Nevertheless, life was great. Things could not of been better. I had nothing to complain about. Life was like watching the ball drop in Times Square on New Year's Eve.; it was music, love, laughter, Confetti; it was a beautiful feeling. I was working, going to school, going to the recording studio to put down tracks for my second record. I was the MC at the Calypso Tent with Bodell and Hazel. I worked with the Mighty Sparrow, My friend Baron, Gypsy, Mello, Darkie Crack Shot Rude Boy, and Old Box. I did shows with Bill Trotman; I worked with the Professor one of the world's best Pan players. I was becoming known in the Calypso world, singing under the name Sherlock. My two songs BULB IN THE SUCKET and

COO YAH MOUTH had a lot of potential, I was told. It just seemed as though everything was going right for me.

I couldn't ask for more. Life was just sweet; still I was very concerned about my change of religion from Baptist to Buddhist, but the way things were going for me at the time, I felt it was a good change. Still I was asking myself; why didn't I come to New York to live before? As the weeks and months of 1985 went by, I made progress in my life. I had my second record in hand and once again, I couldn't get the support or endorsement of a big label like my first record in Los Angles in 1981. They all turned me down. As a result, I had to form my own publishing company in 1981. It was the KARIBBEAN FLAVA MUSIC. I was affiliated with BMI Broadcast Music Incorporated. This time I had to go with a lesser-known label, which didn't help the record sales, at all. I was just putting out and nothing was coming back. I spent almost ten grand on the project. Still, it was a very exciting time for me. I was getting high on life. I felt the curse was lifted, the Voodoo was gone and I was going to be successful. I was going to make it in New York. Little did I know that trouble was around the corner and he had company. It all started when I got hired on at the Battery Park Project.

CHAPTER 34

THE BATTERY PARK INCIDENT

Racism and Bigotry has raised its ugly head again.

In the union, two is a gang and jobs very seldom hire a single welder or fitter, but they will hire a single fitter before they hire a single welder. I 'shaped' the job for weeks at Battery Park and one morning I met Fred there. He was 'shaping' as well. This was sometime in late September of 1985. Fred and I were welders at the Salem Nuclear Power Station in Salem, New Jersey. Fred is Jamaican. He lived in England for a few years. We both lived in the same rooming house in Salem but we didn't have a friendship. We were working buddies, period. In conversation with Fred on that morning I learned that he was experiencing a long period between jobs and was ready to change that. We both got hired that same morning and decided to be a gang. Our agreement was we would alternate on the welding and the fitting. One day I would weld, he would fit; the next day, I would fit and he would weld. You got the drift. We got hired on a Monday and started working the next day. I was truly happy about this because I was tired of jumping from job to job, though I was accumulating benefits. This particular job, however, was going to be nine to ten months and I was thinking that I could save a lot of loot over this period. I could then take some time off and get into radio and develop and improve on what I had learned at broadcasting school. I was feeling good about myself. My self-esteem was sky high and I was very confident that I was going to make it. I was not going to fail. There were several thousand feet of pipe to be installed over fourteen floors, which meant a lot of welding.

The project was a few yards from the Hudson River. The workmen's trailers were a few feet from the edge of the river. Joe Zorn was the general foreman, and a tall, baldhead biker looking Hell's Angels look-alike type of guy was my foreman. There were several other construction companies in the same area. One company had two of my friends and 'homies' working for them Berry Ramsey and my school mate Clinton Modeste. The first day of work, I was asked to get coffee for the men. This is usually what the apprentice does, but I had no problem with that. We were a crew of about eight men. The second day, Fred got the coffee and it appeared to me Jack the foreman was trying to make the only two Blacks in the crew the coffee boys. We did coffee the entire week, taking the orders. To get the coffee, we had to take the elevator all the way to the ground floor to get to the Roach coach. There was always a long line to get to the food. The first week on the job was used to bring piping and fittings to the different floors, which was harder than welding. I had adjusted to this, after working on different jobs in the city. This was just the way it was. The second week, we started welding but we also were asked to get coffee and this was beginning to piss me off. I approached Fred about it. I told him it was wrong for us to be made coffee boys. We were journeymen and we didn't have to get coffee and Danish for the men. It was not in the rules book. If we got coffee, it was supposed to be on a voluntary basis. I told Fred I was not going to get coffee any more.

"Mervyn, I have been out of work for a while and I don't mind doing it," said Fred.

I knew where he was coming from, and knew precisely what to say to him.

"Fred, you are a journeyman; you are not compelled to bring coffee for anybody, but I understand and appreciate your situation and will go along with you."

Mean time, I began to look and listen every morning searching for signs of trouble. I picked up on a few things. The white workers would stand in a circle and talk, while Fred and I would be off on the side in our own brief conversation. He would always go to Jack to get the keys to open the gang boxes. I decided I was not going to do that, either. If I was given the keys, I would open the gang boxes. Fred even started working, while the rest of the crew still stood and talked. This was not good. There were other Black welders working for K

S Construction Company; mostly Jamaicans. I recall Brother Kennedy. He was a nice man. His name is the only one that I remember. They all worked in different areas of the project. Into the third week on the job, Fred and I were still coffee boys for the crew. It was okay for Fred, but I was doing it under protest. The fourth week the shit hit the fan. It was my day to get the coffee. I made a mistake with one order; the guy wanted tea and I brought him coffee My Union brother got very angry and started off on me.

HE said: "Every morning you go for coffee, I always order tea; is that so hard to remember?"

Then he said the following (which was what really pissed me off)

"All you people can do is play basketball and football."

I felt that the remark was racist. I turned to Jack and told him I wanted an apology from the fitter.

The fitter said: "Fuck you. I am not going to give you shit!"

I told Jack the foreman that this was the last day that I was going to get coffee for any one. And meant it. I didn't go down for coffee after that day. Fred continued going for the coffee for the crew. I went for my own.

I read somewhere that A BLACK MAN HAS NO RIGHTS THAT A WHITE MAN IS BOUND TO RESPECT

I proved that to be true on the Battery Park job. After that morning there, was a lot of tension. The white workers started giving me the cold shoulder. What was worse, Fred and I started arguing with each other. A white welder working next to us was making four to five welds a day. Fred was making fifteen. When it was my turn to weld, I would make no more than seven welds, though my welds were quality work. I started disliking Fred because he was bad mouthing me to some of the white workers. One of the white workers told me about it. I didn't tell Fred about it because I didn't want to reveal which one of the white workers told me what he was doing, but it created a lot of tension between us.

Steam Fitters Local 638 worked seven hours a day. Ten four-inch welds a day was a lot of work. On this particular day, Fred made fifteen welds. I asked him to slow down. He told me I couldn't tell him how to work. Then he went to the foreman and told him that I was lazy. The shit hit the fan on that day and we came close to fighting because I called him an Uncle Tom back stabbing motherfucker. After that day, I didn't want to be Fred's partner, but that situation could not change that easily. I had to leave work early on that day. Otherwise Fred and I would have gotten fired for fighting on the job. That is the worst thing that can happen to you on a construction site next to stealing.

The next day we tried to make up, but I was sure I didn't want to be Fred's partner any more. I knew I had to find another job because I was getting some negative vibes from some of the white workers and things that were happening were very disturbing.

One day I went into the trailer. We were finished for the day. I had school that evening. All my clean clothing was on the floor with footprints of a big man all over them. It was then I knew the situation was getting very serious.

I had developed a political awareness for the South African situation and the incarceration of Nelson Mandela and maybe I was angry with white people for their endorsement of the apartheid system in South Africa, even though I knew all whites did not support that system. Nevertheless, I was angry at England, and America for their huge investments in South Africa and at the same time claiming to be democratic countries. I went to work wearing my Free Mandela and Apartheid Must Go buttons, which in retrospect was probably not a wise thing to do. But that was how I felt at the time. With more knowledge about my people and my people's history, I became proud and obstinate, but still I had respect for every one.

Life outside the job was; great my relationship with Ulah was getting better. I didn't want to make the same mistakes I had made in the past. I was determined to be loyal to Ulah. I was determined to become a better man. I was becoming firm in my commitment to Buddha by worshipping and chanting everyday. My self-esteem was way, way up there and I just knew I was going to make it in the Big Apple.

There was still a lot of tension in the air at the job site but I was totally unprepared for what happened next when I got to work that dreadful morning. After changing into my work clothes, I was confronted by a fitter named Willie Herski. The man was at least six feet four inches tall. The trailer was filled. All the Jamaican brothers were there including my partner, Fred as well as a few other white workers.

Herski grabbed me by my collar and pushed me up against the trailer wall and told me he wanted his five dollars. This was a shock to me because I know I didn't owe the man any money. Besides, this was not the way union brothers operated. We were paid in cash. Even if I owed him five dollars, he could have confronted me on payday. He would've gotten his five dollars. But I knew right away it was a set up. Herski and I rode the A train every day from the then Twin Towers. We usually had friendly casual conversation as we sat next to each other on the train. So what the heck was going on?

I told him I didn't recollect borrowing any five dollars from him and even if I did, he didn't have to treat me in this manner. He pulled me to him and then pushed me back against the trailer wall. I was getting angry at this point. It was then I pushed him away from me and I told him I was going to report this matter to the foreman. No one came to my assistance, not even my partner Fred. I sped out of the trailer with Willie in pursuit. I was heading to Joe Zorn's trailer to report the incident. I had to go between two material trailers that were on wheels and was half to the end when I heard Herski say;

"You little nigger, I will kill you."

It was then I got scared. Ahead of me, I saw a small pile of bricks. I picked up two of the bricks. Then I turned around. He kept coming towards me. It was a cold morning. I was still stiff, but I let loose one of the brick. He was a big target. He put his hand up to block his face. The block hit him on his right hand, just above his wrist. I saw blood. That slowed him down. I shot the other brick into his body then ran towards the building, which was under construction. I had lost my focus at this point. I was hot. Instead of going to the Foreman's trailer, I ran into Herski partner, John Shaffer. The shop steward and a few other men were standing next to a parked car. As I was trying to explain what happened to the shop steward, John Shaffer sucker punched me with a right cross to the left side of my face. The blow dazed me. The next thing I knew I was back down on the trunk of the car and three men were hitting me. One I didn't recognize the other two were Shaffer and the biggest shock of all was the fact that the shop steward had joined them. I will never forget his face; the word was he was an alcoholic. I will never forget his cherry red face in my face and his hand at my throat for as long as I live. This was the man who was supposed to be a mediator on the job responsible for settling differences between workers, yet he was one of the men trying to beat the shit out of me. Or were they trying to teach me a lesson?

I was fortunate that my Trinidadian brother, Clinton Modest was on the scene. He was the one that managed to pull those angry men off me. When I was free, I headed straight to Joe Zorn's office. As I got in the door, I heard one worker telling Zorn and I quote

"They just kicked a nigger's ass out there" Unquote. All I said was:

"I am going to call the police."

Zorn came after me. As I was about to leave, he put his arm around me and brought me back inside. He sat me down told me to relax; he gave me a cup of water. I sat in his office for a while. When I calmed down, he told me to go home I would get paid for the day.

This was not about five dollars, this was racism in its most brutal and violent form, and I was thinking about getting even. Some will say I provoked that response, but every one is entitled to their opinion. I say that mentality was there even before I was born.

Thomas Patchel came down the next day. He was the business agent for the Battery Park Area. We had a brief meeting. I don't recall precisely what was discussed, but I remembered he asked me to come in to see him the next day. I never went. Thomas Patchel was running for office at the time. This was bad press for him so I figured not much was going to come from a meeting with him. I never went. I never called. I did go to work the next day. I was not seriously hurt, only had a few lacerations on both of my palms, but my face was hurting from the sucker punch I got from Schaffer. My jaw was also very stiff. Still, I refused to go to the hospital as was suggested by a few people. Others were telling me to file charges against the men involved. I was really thinking about a lawsuit, but I was also thinking about killing Herski, Schaffer, and the shop steward. But I knew I had to find a gun first.

I went to Joe's office to feel the pulse of the work site. Everyone was quiet and low keyed. During the course of the day, I ran into Herski and Schaffer on several occasions. They said nothing to me and I said nothing to them. I felt the tension through my whole body and something inside of me was telling me these two men must die.

The situation was starting to affect my relationship with Ulah. As the days and the weeks went by, it started to deteriorate and none of us was doing anything to stop the flow of the separation that was inevitable.

On the other hand I didn't miss a day of broadcasting school. I even went on to graduate from ATS Announcers Training School in Times Square. I was in a state of shock and disbelief for days and could not believe that I was attacked for five dollars. Every payday, in front of Joe Zorn's trailer, there was always a basket on a table with a request for donations for a sick ailing union brother. It didn't matter that I didn't know the brother, I would always put a ten or a twenty dollar bill in the basket. My thinking was; it could be me one day in need of help.

First of all I didn't know what I was dealing with but knowing the history of the union and the struggle for minority membership, I knew I should have maintained a low profile, but I was deep into the South African issue and the imprisonment of the great freedom fighter, Mr. Nelson Mandela enraged me. I couldn't help myself. I took all that feelings to work with me and I suppose it was showing in the way I carried myself and the things I said.

For instance, when they told me that I could be replaced I would say to them "WHEN I LEAVE, I LEAVE WITH MY DIGNITY AND MY ABILITY" Or when they talked about Black people on welfare or how we are killing each other, I would tell them that white people were responsible for the condition that Black people were in America, that we were the kindest, most forgiving people on the face of the earth. The white union brothers were always dropping words that were laced with bigotry and racism and I would always lash back.

I just couldn't help myself. I didn't see my response to the verbal abuse, as provocation; in retrospect, I think they just wanted to teach me a lesson.

Nevertheless, the incident at Battery Park affected me mentally, and emotionally at the time when things were going great for me. I was in radio broadcasting School. I had my second record on the market. I was living in a brand new house even though it was Ulah's house. But I was her man. And things were going well between us. I was saving my money, working on repairing my credit and telling myself I should've come to New York long before now but after my union brothers attacked me that winter morning in 1985, I was sorry I came to live in New York city, in spite of my accomplishments and my achievements, which to me were huge, by my standards. I was an underachiever who never took any thing seriously, but I will always put my loyalty to Ulah and our time spent together at the top of the list as the noblest thing that I had ever did, second is graduating from radio broadcasting school. I used to be a womanizer, I also used to start a project and never finish.

I will never forget 1978. I was registered at the EL Camino College in Torrance, California as an art student. I went for one week and never went back. Today, I could have been a great artist had I stayed. It was something I wanted to do badly. Why did I withdraw? To this day I don't know. I decided to learn to play the bass guitar. I bought a bass and a small amp and signed up with a small music school in Hollywood. Same action; this time it was for two weeks; had I stayed the course today

I would have been a professional. Why did I quit? Was I a mental case or was I a mad man?

CHAPTER 35

I FOUND A GUN

My friend Winston Simon who lived on Flat Bush Avenue at the time loaned me his 22. After explaining to him what had happened and what I wanted to do, he was supportive but told me he was putting himself in danger if I carried out my plan to commit an act of murder. Simon gave me a crash course on how the gun worked. I became obsessed with the thought of killing those men, but I was also a little bit afraid at the same time. I had hurt my family enough and I didn't want to leave that kind of a legacy behind for them to live with. Plus my mother was alive that would hurt her, but most importantly, my son Chris was a United States Marine and I didn't know how my action would impact him.

I started to dress differently. I bought a plain green Army jacket. I didn't carry a brief case any more; neither did I wear my black leather jacket. I was dressed to kill, literally. On the job, I started stalking Herski and Schaffer. I had the gun in my right pocket. I was not thinking about work. Fred and I were saying little to each other. I was always gone from my work area. Fred was actually welding and fitting at the same time. I would only help him to put the pipe on the Jack Stands, and then I was gone. I didn't tell him about my plans, but he seemed a little sympatatic towards me. Perhaps it was guilt; I don't know.

As the days went by in my search, I found out were Herski and Schaffer were working. I wanted to find them together. I got my wish as I approached the two men one day. I was excited and my heart was pounding. This was it, I said to myself. Herski and Schaffer, together. My hand was in my pocket, holding the gun. My finger was on the trigger, ready to shoot. I was scared and excited at the same time, and when I got close to Herski and Schaffer. They said hi to me and I said hi back at them. The few seconds of greeting made me forget that I had a gun in my pocket. I walked past the two men I wanted to kill. I had the opportunity and just couldn't do it. I gave Simon back his gun the following week. I quit the job. I didn't want to be around Fred and I didn't want to pretend to the white workers that every thing was OK. I was hurt, I was angry, and I had built up a lot of hate within me against my union brothers both Black and white and I couldn't bear to be in the same room as they were.

I found work with a smaller company my friend Leslie Blackman was working with. The company made me feel good. Leslie became an ace pipe fitter. Not surprising; Leslie Graduated from Naprima College in

San Fernando, Trinidad and Tobago. His advancement in the trade was rapid.

In the mean time, Ulah and I separated. To this day, I don't know what happened or how it happened; it just happened. I was out in the cold. Luckily my friend Simon had a bed in his basement on Flatbush Avenue. He allowed me to stay there for a couple weeks. I was going down hill, fast. I started thinking that the curse was back. It was then I gave up Buddha and reverted back to my religion. I started saying my 27 and 51 Psalms. The basement was very quiet. I had a lot of time to think and pray and chant the secret word Leader Martin gave me, but the worst was yet to come.

Simon introduced me to a preacher from Trinidad who had a basement apartment on a street off Church Avenue. I met the man at the house for the viewing of the apartment. He told me someone was on his last week stay. After that I would have the whole basement to myself. I really liked the place and we agreed on three hundred dollars a month. He wanted nine hundred up front.

I remembered giving him nine hundred spanking new one hundred dollar bills. I was anxious to move out of Simon's basement, even though he was not charging me any thing to stay there. There was no bathroom in his basement. I had to climb about twenty steps to urinate. That was rough. So I was happy to move into my own place with a bathroom next to my bedroom. Two days after I moved into my Fairview basement apartment of Church Avenue I had the shock of my life. Ulah's daughter was the tenant who was supposed to be moving out in a week's time. I was very suspicious of her. She was sneaky. She cursed her mother out on Nostrand Avenue and I don't trust any one who disrespects their parents. I was a little angry but since she was getting out in one week, I kept my cool. I had moved in the apartment on a Saturday but by the Thursday of the following week I knew this bitch had to go. She was seeing two men. One was a Calypsonian mate of mine. We did some shows together that year. They called him Rude Boy. The other fellow I didn't know but he sounded as though he was American. I definitely wanted no part of this individual around me. I was emotionally battered. The brutal attack by my so-called union brothers, the break up between Ulah and I had me asking: what's next.

It didn't take long before I found out. The week went by. Jemma was still there. I began to feel uneasy. The following Monday I confronted her about the situation. She told me she was leaving on the weekend. I told her it had better be the weekend. I was very upset. I met Rude Boy during the week and told him to get her out of there because I don't like the girl and what she was about. He told me they were waiting on an apartment to move in. I asked him if he knew about the other man he said no. The second week went by. As we entered the third week, she started avoiding me. The Wednesday of the third week I came home early to find her at the apartment. It was then I confronted her. I knocked on her door. When she opened the door I told her I was fed up with her bullshit. I don't remember what she said. I just snapped. My hands were locked around her neck. I pushed her down on the bed and stood over her. I wanted to beat the shit out of her. I straddled her and was ready to beat her up, but I thank God for preventing me from doing that. I got up off her. I told her stop playing games with me and get the fuck out of here. She left the building. I didn't see her until the next day, when I got off work. The other boy friend was there with her. He didn't say any thing to me, which I found strange. I got home around four PM exhausted, after seven hours of work, and hustling to catch the train to Church Avenue.

I threw myself on the bed. A banging on the door woke me up. When I looked at my watch it was seven thirty. I will never forget it, the banging on the door sounded serious, law enforcement serious. When I opened my door, there were two cops standing in front with Jemma standing behind them. She pointed toward me. I was asked to show my ID. After the police were satisfied that I was who I said I was they promptly asked me to turn around. I was told they were arresting me for attempted rape. I laughed at the charge because sex was the last thing I had on my mind after what I went through with my union brothers of 638 followed by the break up with Ulah.

I was traumatized and devastated by both experiences. No, sex was not on my mind. The cops took me from Fairview and Church to a precinct off Rogers Avenue where I was booked and finger printed. Then I was taken to a downtown jail. While there, I started thinking: the curse was back. I also had thoughts about Ulah and her friends trying to bring me down with their filthy minds and their filthy hands. Still I wasn't scared.

I spent the weekend in jail. I didn't eat a thing. Monday morning, I was brought before the judge smelling kind of funky and tired. I was given a legal aid lawyer. The judge released me on my own recognizance, which was a moral booster to me. When I got back to the apartment, I found out that my two gold chains and my two gold rings were gone. So was Jemma.

I was more happy about the fact that she was gone than the loss of my rings and chains.. Now, I had my apartment to myself. I dropped Buddha like a hot plate and went back to chanting on my word Leader Martin whispered in my ear.   I was going to prayer my way out of this. I started working with Alfa Mechanical. My friend Vernon La Rode was also an employee with the company. Roy, from French Dominica, was the foreman. I would take this brother any where in the world to work with me, he knows pipes. He is a hard worker, and he is fair, not like some of the other Black foremen I worked with in the city; who will never stand up for a brother.   I put my plans for my record distribution on hold, because I wanted to get the hell out of New York. I had money saved up; the only thing that was holding me back was the case. It went on for about three months. In the end, I was vindicated of all charges. I had no doubt that was going to happen. I started making immediate plans to leave New York.   I called my friend, Trevor La Rode, Vernon's brother in Los Angeles and told him I was moving back to California. He and his wife Joan agreed to provide me with housing until I got on my feet. I hold them in very high regard for their kindness.

In November of 1985, I packed up and left New York for good to start a new Life in California. I had no fear of failure. I am a welder. There was work everywhere for welders. Trevor picked me up at the Airport. He and Joan had a room ready for me. They even let me use one of their cars to go job hunting. The first week in California I began to have nightmares about the brutal attack on me at the hands of my union brothers, my break up with Ulah, and the charges brought against me by her daughter. I found work the very first week of my job search. It was then I set up a three-year plan for myself on what I wanted to accomplish. Part of the plan to go back to Trinidad and Tobago and work in Radio Broadcasting

The rest of the story in Part two to be published soon.

QUESTIONS AND ANSWERS: INTERVIEW OF MERVYN V. PATRICK BY KOFI QUAYE

KQ: In part one you make no mention about drugs and alcohol.

Mervyn VP: Simply because I was a clothes person. Drugs and alcohol were not my thing. There was the occasional beer or rum and coke; there was the occasional toke from a joint. I was just trying to fit in.

KQ: Why did you decide to write the book in two parts?

Mervyn VP: Because of a mild heart attack I had on December 21 2005. I spent three days at the University Hospital in Syracuse. After my recovery I told myself

I had better send this first part out before the big one. My children must hear my side of the story.

KQ: What happened?

Mervyn VP: I was working for a maintenance company at the Pharmaceutical Plant in Syracuse New York. My Partner and I were standing in front of a locked gate in a Penicillin area; we had just laid down our tools when a Pen supervisor walk by and saw us standing in front of the gate. She immediately accused us of trying to get in without the proper attire. My partner and I tried to tell her that was not the case but she will not hear any of it. One week later on December 13 2005, I was fired. My partner who happens to be white and female was not. What went down in that week, I suspect was that they certified her for Pen training. I had all the training months before the incident; I knew the do's and don'ts of the Penicillin area, and knew that I was not breaking any rules. The firing really stressed me out; one week later I had a heart attack

Over the last fifteen years, I worked at Bristol of and on. My work was always of a high quality. I knew half the people the other half knew me. Others have broken more serious rules at the plant and have given three days suspension. But I was fired for my first infraction. I ask the question: is it because I am Black?

KQ: What was that experience like for you, I mean the heart attack?

MervynVP: I view it as a near death experience, my blood pressure was 220 [over] 178. Those are stroke numbers. Thanks to the doctors and nurses and support staff, I am alive today.

KQ: What did YOU learn from it?

Mervyn VP: Family and family support. How important it is when you are ill. No one came to see me. I did get calls from my Aunts Cerine, Barbara, and Bernice; that helped to pull me through.

KQ: Did your children call you ?

Mervyn VP: The first day I got to the hospital I called my son Chris, and left a message on his cell phone. He called me later on in the afternoon. I created that situation with my children they have no use for me so I just have to grin and bear it. Still my love for my children will never die.

KQ: When I called you at the hospital you told me you had a Nigerian Liberian as a roommate, what was he like?

Mervyn VP: He was in serious pain, but his wife and children were there to support him. He had two lovely daughters and a son named Perek who is a soccer player. The Liberian was taken to another room. My new roomy was a white man named Jack Clancy; he to was in serious pain, too. I developed a great deal of respect for Mr. Clancy; he has five daughters and a son they gave me maximum respect when they came to visit their father; he introduced me to every one that came to visit him.

Mr. Clancy, get well soon May almighty God bless you and your loved ones regularly and always. The whole scenario with the Nigerian and Mr. Clancy brought tears to my eyes; they were there when their children needed them. I was not there for my children when they needed me, I have to live with that for as long as I live.

"The old people in the island say how you make your bed so you shall sleep."

KQ: In looking back what would you do differently?

Mervyn VP: Take my family everywhere with me; if that can't happen I will not leave them behind.

KQ: What kind of relationship you have with your children today?

Mervyn VP: My two sons in New Jersey; none. As for my legitimate children, I am in contact with Chris, Abu, and my daughter Kurl. My second child Wesley is still staying away.

KQ: What's your thinking on Aids?

Mervyn VP: I believe Aids is a manufactured virus, which is used to restrict the growth and development of Black people. I look at South Africa, and Zimbabwe where was the Aids virus when the whites were in power.

KQ: The war in Iraq.

Mervyn VP: It was a bold and courageous move by the United States, but the world knows it's all about the oil; still we cannot give the impression that's the reason why we are there. It was a master chess move. America is a super power and she is just acting, as a Super Power should.

KQ: If you die and were to come back a white man who would it be?

Mervyn VP: It will be a toss up between Will Rogers, and Billy Graham. Will Rogers said he never met a man he didn't like. Billy Graham stuck to his story, he never deviated. We all know what his story is.

KQ : If you die and were to come back a Black man who would it be?

Mervyn VP: That's easy. Dr Eric Williams, the father of the nation of Trinidad and Tobago, the country of my birth. My second choice would be Kamaladin Mohamed who was loyal to Dr Williams in every way. Mr. Mohamed should have been the successor to Dr Williams; he should have been the next Prime Minister of Trinidad and Tobago, but he wasn't for obvious reasons.

KQ: Why did you decide to settle in Syracuse?

Mervyn VP: Because my mother is buried here, and she was my best friend. So is my brother who was a wonderful brother; he was the first person to bring the Caribbean Carnival Festival to Syracuse.

BOOKS BY KOFI QUAYE

CRISIS IN THE FAMILY [HERITAGE BOOKS]

This book tells an too common a story: the cross-cultural conflicts most immigrants face virtually everywhere they go. Everyone who has experienced the immigrant life has dealt with the challenge of coping with life in a country where almost everything-language, culture, religion -differs from what they know or were nurtured with. An African family in New York finds itself in the throes of change; some members of the family welcome the change; others resist it. The result is nothing short of a nightmare.

WHEN THE IMMIGRANT'S DREAM TURNS INTO A NIGHTMARE [HERITAGE BOOKS]

An up close and personal look at the problems, traumas, tragedies, challenges as well as the rewards of immigration, emigration and migration as told by people who have experienced them. These are the stories you won't read in the newspapers or see on television. The increasing incidence of suicides in Third World immigrant communities in Europe, North America, Australia, etc, unexplained premature deaths, the disappearance of men and women who are never found, the horror stories of immigrants exploited by unscrupulous employers and criminals.

JOJO IN NEW YORK [Macmillan]

A young African arrives in New York with preconceived notions about life in America; he thinks he knows enough from watching television and reading magazines and books. The real deal is a far cry from what he knows. Only his 'mother wit'-common sense-saves him from the danger that stalks him.

Books may be ordered from:
HERITAGE BOOKS
P.O. BOX 46
Syracuse, NY, 13210
Tel: 315-471-7899
E-mail: info@mysteek.com

Mervyn V. Patrick

Kofi Quaye

About the Author
and the Collaborator

Both the author, Mervyn Vincent Patrick, and collaborator, Kofi Quaye, reside in Syracuse, NY, and share many things in common, not the least of which is the fact that they are both immigrants, and artists, of sorts.

Kofi Quaye, originally from Ghana, is an internationally recognized author of several books of fiction and non-fiction. His books focus mostly on the 'immigrant experience' and include JOJO IN NEW YORK published by Macmillan Publishing Co., England, CRISIS IN THE FAMILY [HERITAGE BOOKS, NY,] FREE FROM DEATH ROAD, [HERITAGE BOOKS, NY] WHEN THE IMMIGRANT'S DREAM TURNS INTO A NIGHTMARE [IMPRINT BOOKS, NY]

To Kofi Quaye, collaborating in writing the book was an 'exercise in nostalgia.' It is a book which essentially reflects his own experiences in terms of growing up in a cultural ambience in Africa where belief in ancient religions, customs, rituals and traditions exists side by side with Christianity, to the confusion and bewilderment of men, women and youth who don't know which one to accept or reject.

To Mervyn V. Patrick, writing the book was a labor of love; he wanted to tell his side of the story, to his children and others who want to know the real truth about his experiences as an immigrant, the challenges he faced, the obstacles he overcame and the ultimate price he paid.